TO CHANGE A CHILD:
A Report on
the Institute For
Developmental Studies

TO CHANGE A CHILD:
A Report on
the Institute For
Developmental Studies
By Fred Powledge

Published in cooperation with the
Anti-Defamation League of B'nai B'rith
by **Quadrangle Books,** Chicago

PREFACE

Probably the most important consideration in contemplating the education of the disadvantaged child is to recognize that the problem is not solved. In our society, it is always a simpler step to initiate a program than it is to make a critical analysis of initial results, and to follow through on the implications of the analysis. It must also be recognized that there are many levels of real ambivalence that exist with respect to almost all change—for the schools have become a major focal point for social change.

Successful educational programs for children will be composed of many components, but one of the most important will be extra-educational: it will have to do with the increasing and continuing experience of equality of opportunity by all members of a family and of a community at all points in the life cycle. There will be greater pressure on the school to prepare *all* people for functioning in a highly complex technological society.

The impetus for this book came from the Anti-Defamation League of B'nai B'rith and its Program Director, Mr. Oscar Cohen, who believed that maximum communication of existing information is a necessary aspect of formulating any approach to these problems facing the schools. I am pleased that we at the Institute for Developmental Studies were able

v

to cooperate, and I am grateful to Mr. Fred Powledge for producing such a lucid and well-written account of the area which the Institute addresses as well as aspects of its program in early childhood education.

The Institute for Developmental Studies is a multi-disciplinary organization. It thus enjoys the opportunity to cut across the different disciplines in the human and social sciences, and to bring to bear on curriculum and educational organization the knowledge and research findings from a variety of fields. This is a difficult process, and not one which leads to speedy solutions to the complex problems of either children's learning processes on the one hand, or urban education on the other.

The current vogue in education places a great deal of faith in psychological testing results as measures of program success. This faith may be well placed, but it tends to overshadow another worthwhile source of evaluation, reports of individual teachers. No matter what test results indicate, the teachers still see children who are stimulated in the areas of curiosity and initiative. It is the teachers, themselves, who are responsible for much of the children's heightened curiosity and initiative, and it is precisely these two characteristics that the usual testing in schools does not measure.

Two other points should be noted. One is that the Institute teachers work in a relatively advantageous setting. Class size is not overwhelming to either teacher or child. The teacher has time to prepare and evaluate. She has the help of specialists readily available, and she enjoys the benefits of continuous supervision from a supervisor who is not overburdened by an unmanageable number of teachers to supervise. The teacher participates in regularly conducted in-service training activities.

The second point is that social groups are heterogeneous.

VI

That is, while we may speak of the "disadvantaged" or the "middle-class" as though they were homogeneous groups, this is not in fact the case. Within each group are great variations in family organization, background, and personal experience, even though the groups so identified have a degree of homogeneity in education and occupation of main breadwinner, which is the basis for the social class designation.

I should like to stress that the description contained in this book is of the *current* Institute program, which is an evolving one. A great deal of change is to be anticipated, both as a result of the incorporation of past experience and of new knowledge, and in response to changing social conditions and to the changes produced by the achievements of previous programs. It is hoped that the general information communicated here, however, will be helpful as an orientation to work on the problems explicated.

MARTIN DEUTSCH

TO CHANGE A CHILD:
A Report on
the Institute For
Developmental Studies

The disadvantaged child. The mere pronunciation of those three words stirs up a variety of reactions, of emotions, in a variety of people. To some, it automatically means *the black child.* Or it may mean the child who speaks Spanish, or the child who was born of an Appalachian mountain family. Or the child of a home that has been broken, or one in which there never was a father.

Perhaps to almost everyone the phrase means *the child who doesn't have a chance,* or, worse, *the child who may never have a chance.* Because of this "disadvantage," a disadvantage that is so obvious, so easily determined and acknowledged so early in his life, the child who finds himself in this category is a child who is destined to remain disadvantaged. The American Dream is not for him.

This nation may very well be a place where parents can tell their children that everybody has a chance to grow up and become President, but the parents of the disadvantaged child know that to tell their children this is to play a cruel joke. They know too well that their child's future already has been predicted and, to a great extent, determined. It has been predicted and determined by the same machines, the same computers and systems, that someday may deny that child a job. These parents know, as do educators and economists and politicians, that the disadvantaged child soon may become the alienated student, and then he may become the high-school dropout, and then the unemployed adult.

1

But in America this is not supposed to happen. There *is* supposed to be an American Dream, and that dream is supposed to be accessible to everyone, regardless of his poverty or his affluence. It is part of the tradition of this country—or is it part of the mythology?—that when situations like this arise, and when, through curious accidents or planned campaigns of publicity, or political commitment, or crisis, they reach the attention of the nation, and then start to prey on its conscience, then somebody does something about them.

So we have Project Head Start. So we have a war on poverty. We have a civil rights movement that, once its initial graphic points had been made on the battlefields of the Deep South, has tried to speak louder and more clearly about the need to interpret a minority's troubles in terms of economics, in terms of disadvantage, and in terms of power. So it may be argued that somebody *is* trying to do something about the situation. Somebody is trying to do something about the disadvantaged child.

Thousands of people are trying to do something. Surely no third-grade teacher in a slum school could go through her working day, now, thinking of her students in the comfortable ways her predecessor may have thought of them. Surely the nation has realized by now that it means nothing (except to quote the Bible out of context) to say you have the poor with you always. All across the nation thoughtful people are trying to construct programs to do something about the disadvantaged child and the other victims of poverty and discrimination.

They do this because they are ashamed at the treatment that the disadvantaged child has received in the past, or because they simply want to do the right thing, or because they fear the statistics that they digest with each morning's newspaper—the predictions of joblessness, the promises of automation, the numbers of people who engaged in yesterday's race riot. They do this, some of them, because they are touched by the thought of an innocent child's being cheated out of something that rightfully belongs to him. So they start their programs, and they hope that their programs will do some good. Sometimes they see progress; often they see failure. More often they see success, but success of such limited nature that their programs are de-emphasized, forgotten, and finally discarded.

The Institute for Developmental Studies

It was not only predictable, but also entirely fitting and proper, that the behavioral sciences should start to play important roles in the effort to do something about the disadvantaged child. With a problem so pathetic, so obviously destructive of innocent children, it was no wonder that scientists began, many years ago, to try to find out why children were disadvantaged and to see if means could be developed for helping them.

In some cases, the scientists conducted their investigation through specially-constructed schools. There they could easily observe their disadvantaged students at work; they could better diagnose the problems that those children brought with them to the classroom, and they could try out their hypothetical solutions in a setting that closely resembled the natural scientist's laboratory. In almost all of the research and experimental projects, the behavioral scientists have accepted the idea that compensatory change

3

should be brought to the child at an early age—certainly before he is old enough to attend the first grade, and probably before he is old enough for kindergarten.

In the United States, the pioneering agency in this sort of study in early childhood education was the Institute for Developmental Studies, a Division of the Department of Psychiatry of New York Medical College, now affiliated with the New York University School of Education. It was founded in 1958 as a research and demonstration unit that could draw on the offerings of a number of disciplines, not just psychiatry. The Institute's own literature explains, in general terms, what it seeks to do:

> The Institute is engaged in a long-range investigation of the developmental, psychological, and social determinants of learning and intelligence, with particular emphasis on the role of environmental influences. Approximately twenty-two separate Institute studies comprise a mutually reinforcing cycle of basic and applied research, demonstration programs, and their evaluation. For example, research studies in cognition, social background, and personality have been translated into therapeutic classroom procedures, which in turn have been evaluated within the Institute's major demonstration project, namely, the preschool-through-third-grade enrichment program. The enrichment program has ultimately yielded new hypotheses that have been referred to the research program for further exploration.[1]

What this means is that the Institute is not an exercise in ivory-tower postulating, although everything it does is subjected to the same sort of academic scrutiny that goes into research in the natural sciences. Neither is the Institute a store-front center for slum activism, although it *is* physically located in a store-front (a modern one, in Greenwich Village, close to its parent institution) and, until the summer of 1966, it was situated on the edge of Harlem. The Institute, because its purpose is to conduct a "mutually reinforcing cycle of ba-

---

1. Institute for Developmental Studies, "Annual Report 1965," p. 7.

sic and applied research, demonstration programs, and their evaluation," has to be both a center for research and a center for action programming, and that is one of the things that makes it so interesting.

Basic research at the Institute may show that lower-class children come to school lacking the fundamental intimacies with, say, the alphabet that their more middle-class colleagues bring with them. Those at the Institute who are concerned primarily with applied research may design a device that they feel may help the disadvantaged child to understand and enjoy the alphabet more. (The device is soon to be mass-produced, under the name, "Letter Form Board," by Houghton Mifflin Publishers, Boston.)

Then the board might be introduced in the Institute's demonstration program, which is conducted in the New York City school system.

But it is not merely introduced and then forgotten. Those at the Institute whose preoccupation is with evaluation will watch the Letter Form Board; they will watch the children who use it. They will modify it if it needs modification. They will try it out on other groups of children—middle-class children, for instance—to see if its usefulness is limited, or if it might be a valuable learning tool for all children. Finally, once it has been conceived, built, evaluated, modified, tested and retested, the device might become part of the curriculum that the Institute feels will be of assistance to disadvantaged children. But even then its value is subject to review, modification and improvement.

This sort of scrutiny is not reserved for machines and teaching devices. The scientific method is applied, too, to every hypothesis that is raised by the Institute, whether it concerns the quality and quantity of conversation that should be carried on between the teacher and her pupils, the

5

usefulness of construction paper as a teaching aid, or the desirability of better insulation in the classroom's walls.

The constant plugging away at this "mutually reinforcing cycle" might seem, to some, a gigantic waste of money and time and human resources at the very moment when the nation is most receptive to the idea of doing something about the disadvantaged child—at the moment when politicians and school boards, private citizens and city councils are most willing to spend money and start programs. To some, it is wrong to allow even the slight delay that might be demanded by further research, testing and retesting, evaluation and re-evaluation. But to the scientists at the Institute for Developmental Studies, the search for the answers to disadvantaged childhood is far from over. They are extremely skeptical of "get-enrichment-quick" ideas.

Many of the answers to the problems of disadvantaged children appear to be close at hand. For instance, the Institute seems to have developed a useful set of strategies for reaching one of its major goals—finding out "how much intensive enriched education will be necessary before one sees significant advances maintained." Though there are no magic numbers, there are solid, educated guesses now available on what an optimum, practical pupil-to-teacher ratio should be, and even on what the per-student cash outlay should be in an enriched pre-school program.

But for the Institute for Developmental Studies, none of the answers will be worth very much without a basic rearrangement of the institution of education itself—a reclassification, review, reassessment of our traditional ways of dealing with the disadvantaged child, and a new commitment to doing the job well. Therefore it is not surprising to learn that Dr. Martin Deutsch, the director of the Institute, and his colleagues insist that any understanding of the problems of the disadvantaged child, and any attempt to correct those problems, be preceded by an understanding of the confusing, complex, and tragically inadequate institution that lies just on the other side of the schoolhouse door.

The Status Quo

It is a fact of life, a fact that scientists, educators and ordinary citizens now are comprehending more than ever before, that the American public school system is, almost by definition, an agency of discrimination. One important reason for this is the simple fact that the institution of education, which is supposed to free men's minds from the snarls of bureaucracy and wooden thinking, is itself, in fact, a foremost example of just that sort of thinking. It perpetuates, rather than helps to change, the *status quo*. As Dr. Deutsch has written:

In a sense, the institution of education—the school—*is* the *status quo*. It often operates through huge politically oriented bureaucracies that continually inhibit its potential for change and for developing strategies for meeting social crises such as those inherent in the new urban America. These bureaucracies are often so large that introduction of meaningful change, even when agreed on by the higher echelons, is limited by the clogging of communications channels with paper, red tape, and assorted other artifacts, and by the constraints under which the average classroom teacher operates.

Somehow, this great gap in the educational hierarchy, separating the educator and his concept from the classroom teacher and her idea, creates a discontinuity that results in much wasted energy and distortion of effort. A clear educational philosophy can come best from educators who are free enough from bureaucracy to communicate with the classroom teacher as a full professional, and to attenuate the burden of the past while setting up new relationships with the human sciences.[2]

2. Martin Deutsch, "Social and Psychological Perspectives on the Development of the Disadvantaged Learner," *Journal of Negro Education*, (Summer 1964), p. 234.

The degree of self-criticism that is currently rampant among educators confirms Dr. Deutsch's argument. In an institution that is so entwined with bureaucracy, and so historically rigid, a significant amount of internal condemnation comes to the surface with surprising frequency. Some of those who indulge in this self-criticism see the public school institution as too much of a creature of elective and appointive politics; some see it as choking in the grip of the teacher-training institutions; others see the age of educators as a major problem.

One fairly young school administrator, who was attending one of the Institute's frequent week-long "extra-mural training work conferences," had this comment on what she had seen: "I'm impressed mostly, I suppose, by the youth of the Institute people. They're all so *young!* I guess it's just harder for the administrators who're older, and who've been around longer, to accept these new ideas.

"Education's tough enough as it is. When you get to talking about this sort of *change,* it must seem like more than some of these older people can take."

It is true that educators in recent years have developed, by themselves, an imposing series of new methods of teaching, new machines for assisting in the learning process, new tests to measure the ability of the child when he enters the classroom and to ascertain the effectiveness of the education to which he has been exposed. But these techniques, like so much of what has been produced by the American public school, suffer from the same overriding and fatal flaw from which the entire educational institution suffers: They are designed with only the middle-class child in mind.

The school has been planned, constructed, and operated essentially as a middle-class institution. The questions it asks, the answers it demands, the approaches it takes, the

8

books it chooses, the standards it imposes, and the people it employs are virtually all middle-class in origin, in orientation, in language, in gesture, and in the expectations they convey to the children who inhabit the school. The life for which they are trying to prepare their students—the life that is so fondly mentioned by commencement speakers from one end of the nation to the other—is a middle-class life.

None of this is necessarily evil in itself. This does not mean that middle-classness should be condemned as something to be avoided and scorned because it is alien to the best interests of the nation. Indeed, it may be said that middle-class life and expectations of middle-class life are important components of the American Dream.

But it does mean that American children—and this includes all classes of American children—attend public schools that are basically middle-class institutions, institutions that do all their measuring against middle-class standards, institutions that define failure and success, and prescribe rewards and punishment, on the basis of middle-class rules. Thus, by definition, they are institutions that—to the child who is not equipped to cope with middle-class methods and concepts, who comes into the classroom with no previous knowledge of what middle-class America seeks, demands, or even is—are strange and foreign places.

Much, even perhaps all, of the work of the Institute for Developmental Studies is based in whole or in part upon the recognition of this tremendously significant disparity between the orientation of the poor, or lower-class, or disadvantaged child and the orientation of the school that society has charged with the task of educating him. It is the aim of the Institute to find ways to abbreviate or eliminate this disparity through the interrelated techniques of research, application, and evaluation. The Institute wants to motivate the institution of education to assume more responsibility for exposing the disadvantaged child to the middle-class attributes that are missing from his own home environment—not to force-feed him with those attributes, but to at least enable him to understand and cope with them. And the Institute seeks to motivate the schools to recognize that the disadvantaged child has attributes of his own that are valuable, that are worthy of consideration and respect, and that may be incorporated in a curriculum that introduces the lower-class child to the educational process and that encourages his interest in it.

The question might be raised, then, "But isn't it *right* for the disadvantaged child to be forced into a middle-class situation? If the lower-class child is going to learn how to compete for the American Dream, isn't it essential that he learn the rules of middle-class society from the beginning?" One answer to that might be that, unless the rules of the game are changed, it doesn't matter; that the disparity between the two cultures—the child's and his school's—is so great that his chances of learning to respect or even to understand the rules of middle-class society in any meaningful manner are all but hopeless.

For it is not just a matter of comparing the environment of the lower-class child with the environment of the school. A third factor—the environment of the middle-class child who may attend that same school—must be taken into consideration. It is for *him*, and not for the disadvantaged child, that the I.Q. tests are written, the spelling bees are held, and the report cards are graded. And he comes to school with a curriculum already built into his brain. From his birth, the middle-class child has been schooled in the same sort of things that the school later will expect him to learn. He knows the alphabet, or most of it; he knows the value of speech, and he has been encouraged since birth to carry on conversations, of sorts, with adults and with his peers. He knows colors, and he has easy access to crayons and construction paper. His parents buy him books, just as they have bought him reading materials ever since he was old enough to listen to a story being told. "Middle-class homes," said Dr. Deutsch in a recent article, "have a so-called 'hidden curriculum' that typically does an effective job of preparing middle-class children to enter school. This doesn't happen in lower-class impoverished homes."[3]

When the middle-class child enters the first grade or kindergarten, he does not typically suffer from the same shock of changed environments that may induce something akin to a trauma in a lower-class child. School is a *continuation* of the atmosphere that has prevailed all along in the middle-class home. To the child from such a home, the teacher is another interested adult who asks questions and who may be consulted for answers; the crayons and paints and books and toys are a lot like those at home.

The middle-class child enters the school already with experience in success and failure; the lower-class child may not. And both the middle- and the lower-class child have their placement and their progress measured by the same intelligence and achievement tests, tests that quite likely are culturally and economically biased in the favor of the middle-class child.

And what does the disadvantaged child bring with him?

He brings a background almost totally different from that of the middle-class child, a background that only hinders him as he attempts to cope with the new environment, the middle-class orientation, of the school. He brings a whole series of

3. Martin Deutsch, "What We've Learned About Disadvantaged Children," *Nation's Schools*, (April 1965), pp. 50-51.

qualities, which can only be referred to by the majority society as deficiencies. One of the most important of those deficiencies is retardation in the vital area of reading. Dr. Deutsch has estimated that

Currently, forty to seventy per cent of the total school population in our twenty largest cities consists of children from marginal economic and social circumstances. By the time these children reach junior high school, sixty per cent are retarded in reading by one to four years. We know that this academic retardation carries with it a much broader social retardation and that it represents a tremendous loss to America of very needed resources.

It is a simple fact that unskilled jobs are decreasing rapidly and that it will be increasingly necessary for people to enter the job market highly prepared to perform skilled tasks. This is well-nigh impossible for people who are alienated from school at an early age. Thus current social necessities demand attention to the educational process, and especially to the participation in it of the children from the most deprived circumstances.[4]

The lower-class child also brings with him a history of deprivation and discrimination that quite naturally limits his ability to become a contributing part of the middle-class educational experience. Much of the work of the Institute for Developmental Studies has been directed at isolating these components of deprivation and discrimination, on the theory that little of consequence can be done about their effects on the child until they are individually and collectively discovered and dealt with. Most of them would be obvious to any thoughtful observer; it has been the Institute's task to isolate and analyze those components in a scientific manner, so that attempts might be made to deal with them.

The disadvantaged child comes, for instance, from a home environment that is physically crowded. There is little privacy. He and all his brothers and sisters and parents may live

4. Martin Deutsch, "Social and Psychological Perspectives on the Development of the Disadvantaged Learner," *op. cit.*, p. 232.

in a two-room apartment with only curtains separating the rooms. He may have no place to study that he can call his own, no shelf for his books, no reading lamp. If, as in many cases, he comes from a broken home, he may suffer psychologically from the absence of the symbol of maleness; also, because his mother may have to work, he may be thrust early in life into the responsibility of caring for younger brothers and sisters, and he may seem old beyond his years, and tired and humorless. He may have only one hot meal each day, and this may contribute to his lack of energy.

For the disadvantaged child who is a Negro, there is more. He brings with him a life in which racial discrimination is a daily event, and in which the memories of slavery are freshened by a society that maintains a caste system with well-delineated inferior and superior castes; and the salient perceptions are too frequently carried over into the classroom.

This disadvantaged child brings, too, a life in which chronic economic insecurity is a matter of fact. He also may come from a home in which the adults answer his questions with one-syllable "Yeses" or "Noes." As Dr. Deutsch put it: "Adults are resource people. In a middle-class home, a child asks and asks and asks. And he gets answers. This is not true in all homes." And he adds:

Related to the whole issue of the adult-child dynamic in establishing a basis for the later learning process is the ability of the child to use the adult as a source for information, correction and the reality testing involved in problem-solving and the absorption of new knowledge. When free adult time is greatly limited, homes vastly overcrowded, economic stress chronic, and the general educational level very low—and, in addition, when adults in our media culture are aware of the inadequacy of their education—questions from children are not encouraged, as the adults might be embarrassed by their own limitations and anyway are too preoccupied wtih the business of just living and surviving. In the child's formulation of concepts of the world, the ability to formulate questions is an essential step in data gathering. If questions are not en-

13

couraged or if they are not responded to, this is a function which does not mature.[5]

A function which does not mature. That, in the estimation of Dr. Deutsch and others at the Institute, is what happens in the mental processes of many disadvantaged children. Functions which are inherent in the child, but which are not stimulated, do not mature, and so the lower-class children enter school, says Dr. Deutsch, "already behind their middle-class counterparts in a number of skills highly related to scholastic achievement."

The lower-class child enters school deficient in the ability to remember things. "It is adults who link in the past and the present by calling to mind prior shared experiences," Deutsch has written. "The combination of the constriction in the use of language and in shared activity results, for the lower-class child, in much less stimulation of the early memory function."[6]

Similarly, the lower-class child brings a conception of *time* that is at variance with the conceptions of time that are employed, and taken for granted, in middle-class homes and in schoolrooms. The teacher may parcel the school day into a number of time periods, alloting a certain number of minutes for each of a variety of activities. Studies at the Institute have shown that the lower-class child is simply not as prepared for this sort of categorization as is his middle-class contemporary. And, if the school does not in some way take this deficiency into consideration, the child will go through kindergarten, the first grade, the second grade, and further, never having mentally filed away (or "interiorized," as behavioral scientists put it) this vitally important conception—a concep-

5. Martin Deutsch, "The Disadvantaged Child and the Learning Process: Some Social, Psychological and Developmental Considerations," in A. H. Passow (editor), *Education in Depressed Areas*, New York: Teachers College Bureau of Publications, (1963), p. 173.
6. *Ibid.*, p. 171.

tion on which so much of what he is supposed to learn later is based.

The lower-class child will not be as prepared, either, for the system of rewards and punishment, or the traditions of success and failure, that are observed by the school. Dr. Deutsch has pointed out that one of the areas

in which the lower-class child lacks pre-school orientation is the well-inculcated expectation of reward for performance, especially for successful task completion. The lack of such expectation, of course, reduces motivation for beginning a task and, therefore, also makes less likely the self-reinforcement of activity through the gaining of feelings of competence. In these impoverished, broken homes there is very little of the type of interaction seen so commonly in middle-class homes, in which the parent sets a task for the child, observes its performance, and in some way rewards its completion. Neither, for most tasks, is there the disapproval which the middle-class child incurs when he does not perform properly or when he leaves something unfinished. Again, much of the organization of the classroom is based on the assumption that children anticipate rewards for performance and that they will respond in these terms to tasks which are set for them.[7]

Also, writes Deutsch,

The lower-class child does not have the same coping mechanisms for internalizing success or psychologically surviving failure in the formal learning setting. If the lower-class child starts to fail, he does not have the same kind of operationally significant and functionally relevant support from his family or community—or from the school—that his counterpart has.

Further, because of the differences in preparation, he is more likely to experience failure....The school becomes a place which makes puzzling demands, and where failure is frequent and feelings of competence are subsequently not generated. Motivation decreases, and the school loses its effectiveness.[8]

And, Deutsch adds, gradual but continual failure may have the result of alienating the lower-class child from the school

7. *Ibid.*, p. 172.
8. Martin Deutsch, "Social and Psychological Perspectives on the Development of the Disadvantaged Learner," *op. cit.*, pp. 237-238.

and from what it stands for—the device by which the doors of opportunity, the doors leading to the American Dream, may be opened.

There is another group of abilities in which the disadvantaged child is likely to be deficient. These are the very devices for receiving stimulation—devices which, again, are commonplace in the middle-class child who has brought a "hidden curriculum" with him. They include the tactile, verbal and visual abilities.

The lower-class child has less of an opportunity to receive those stimulations than does his more affluent counterpart. He has much less exposure, in his earliest years, to toys, pencils, crayons, puzzles, blocks of wood, stuffed animals. He does not learn to associate a purple crayon with the color purple or with the sound of the word "purple," or with the abstract concept of purple, because in so many instances there is just no purple crayon available. A more affluent child will have a roomful of toys and blocks that are scientifically designed to bring him gratification and knowledge; he will learn the concept of speed from his toy racing set, the concepts of color, size and shape from his collection of brightly-painted stacking rings, the concept of three-dimensional objects from his box of Lincoln Logs or Lego System blocks. In addition, he will be welcome most of the time in a kitchen that is full of pots, pans, coffee cans, and muffin tins, and there he may further explore the worlds of shape, size, weight, touch, softness, hardness, color, and mass.

He will have access to his father's toolbox, and perhaps to the mysteries of the automobile in the garage. He may have a pet, a dog or a cat, or guinea pigs, turtles, or white rats, and from them he will receive additional stimulation and development of his tactile, visual, and verbal resources. And there will be a library of books, books which his parents are for-

16

ever reminding him are filled with knowledge, and which have pictures, many of them, and colorful jackets. Parents, and adults of any sort, are more likely to be on hand in the home of the middle-class child, and they are going to be more likely to stop what they are doing and answer the child's questions and to provide his eyes, his ears, and his fingertips with new and gradually more complex stimulations.

And there is a chance that the affluent child will have fewer brothers and sisters than will the disadvantaged child, and thus his parents will have more time to spend on what the scientists call "individuation," the expenditure of adult time on an individual child's problems, desires, and education.

The disadvantaged child has much less of all of this than his middle-class contemporary, and, in some cases, he has virtually none of it. Says Deutsch:

In the [disadvantaged] child's home, there is a scarcity of objects of all types, but especially of books, toys, puzzles, pencils, and scribbling paper. It is not that the mere presence of such materials would necessarily result in their productive use, but it would increase the child's familiarity with the tools he'll be confronted with in school....

Visually, the urban slum and its overcrowded apartments offer the child a minimal range of stimuli. There are usually few, if any, pictures on the wall, and the objects in the household, be they toys, furniture, or utensils, tend to be sparse, repetitious, and lacking in form and color variations. The sparsity of such objects and the lack of diversity of home artifacts which are available and meaningful to the child, in addition to the unavailability of individualized training, give the child few opportunities to manipulate and organize the visual properties of his environment and thus perceptually to organize and discriminate the nuances of that environment....The sparsity of manipulable objects probably also hampers the development of these functions in the tactile area. For example, while these children have broomsticks and usually a ball, possibly a doll or a discarded kitchen pot to play with, they don't have the different shapes and colors and sizes to manipulate which the middle-class child has in the form of blocks which are bought just for him, or even in the variety of sizes and shapes of cooking utensils which might

17

be available to him as playthings.[9]

Another difference between the lower-class child and the middle-class child appears to be in the disadvantaged child's tendency to shy away from verbal and other sorts of assistance when it finally is offered to him by a sympathetic adult or a dedicated teacher.

The conversations most likely to be heard in the home of a lower-class child are conversations that are not directed at the child. They are conversations about racial discrimination, economic insecurity, and the hardships of just living in poverty in the midst of a land of plenty. The child, then, learns "very quickly to tune out," according to Vera P. John, of the Institute for Developmental Studies.

"Instead of listening, they learn not to listen," she adds. And when this child gets to school, where the tradition is to shower him with information, his reaction is to tune out even more—to try to ignore the bits of information that, for him, are so complex, so great in number, and so high in frequency. So he tunes out. And, perhaps, sooner or later, he drops out. And he becomes another casualty of the educational system.

It should not be difficult to recognize that deficiencies such as these, found on such a large scale, cannot correctly be attributed to brain damage, birth defects, disease, or myths of racial inferiority or superiority. They can be attributed only to the attempts that society has made—and successful attempts, whether they were made consciously or unconsciously —to withhold certain vital, fundamental experiences and concepts from the lower-class child, so that his life, when compared with the better-off child, appears less complete. Dr. Deutsch refers to this as "stimulus deprivation" and "environmental disadvantage." They are negative factors that easily can destroy a child's motivation to do something once

---

9. Martin Deutsch, "The Disadvantaged Child and the Learning Process: Some Social, Psychological and Developmental Considerations," *op. cit.*, pp. 167, 170.

he enters a public school, especially when the school is predicated, from kindergarten to diploma, on middle-class American traditions, habits, and beliefs.

It should not be difficult to recognize that the child who comes to school with these deficiencies, and who is confronted with the newness and strangeness of the school, and who above all is not prepared to respond to the school's stimuli in the accepted way, soon will be a child for whom the school experience is not relevant. Deutsch has written that when the lower-class child who is the victim of such a situation enters school, "initial failures are almost inevitable, and the school experience becomes negatively rather than positively reinforced. Thus a child's experiences in school do nothing to counteract the invidious influences to which he is exposed in his slum, and sometimes segregated, neighborhood."[10]

What will happen if children are allowed to continue this tradition of entering the schools unprepared and leaving them even more unprepared, or dropping out along the line, is a matter of prime concern not only for educators, but for economists and historians as well. Some observers might be offended at the suggestion that there is a direct connection between the schools' neglect of disadvantaged children and the frequency and incidence of street riots. But surely everyone who is familiar with the situation must agree that continued neglect will have a definite bearing on the labor market.

It is almost beside the point, however, to offer statistical arguments for eliminating the spectre of a disadvantaged childhood. The horror of the words alone should be enough to convince the nation that the job needs to be done, and that it needs to be done as quickly and efficiently as possible.

---

10. *Ibid.*, p. 163.

The Most Promising Agency

It is safe to say that most observers of the situation agree that the place to start is in the school itself. Years of coping with the continuing controversy over racial segregation in the North has led these observers to reject any alternative suggestion as an attempt by white society to sidestep the issue. They have become extremely wary of the argument that, while it is true that the three major demands of the victims of discrimination are jobs, housing, and education, nothing may be done about any one of the three unless and until something is done about the others. School boards have been particularly shortsighted in adopting this argument. They have been far too prone to issue statements that say nothing can be done about education until improvements are made in jobs and housing.

By now, though, there seems to be in both the North and the South a general agreement among intelligent people that what is done in the school, regardless of what is done in other areas, can have a great and lasting effect on the overall progress that will be made by the Negro in Los Angeles and Jackson, the Puerto Rican in the Bronx, the Mexican in Chicago, the Indian in Minnesota, and the poor white in Appalachia. It is obvious that the school is the most important single channel for prospective change. Writes Dr. Deutsch, in support of the concept of early childhood education:

The most promising agency for providing environmental compensations is the school; it is through this institution, which reaches every child, that the requisite stimulation for facilitating learning, psychological maturation, and acculturation can be most efficiently organized and programmed. But it is now estimated that up to sixty per cent of lower-class children are retarded two years or more in reading by the time they leave the elementary school....

The failure of the educational institution to overcome the children's

20

environmentally-determined handicaps results too often in early failure, increasing alienation, and an increasingly larger gap between the lower-class and middle-class youngsters as they progress through school. In other words, the intellectual and achievement differences between lower-class and middle-class children are smallest at the first grade level, and tend to increase through the elementary school years.[11]

There are some critics of the educational system who scoff at the suggestion that the system itself can do anything that is both meaningful and right. Schools are run, by and large, by politicians, they argue, and to a politician what is right is not necessarily the first consideration. Schools are also run—their policies conceived, their decisions made—by bureaucrats, by people who know little about education, by people who do not want to get involved in controversies, by people to whom petty office politics are a part of the daily routine. A public school system still is not a comfortable haven for adventurers or innovators, or for those who hold any but the most conventional, most currently fashionable philosophies of child education. And while the institutions that train the people who run the schools have been indicted repeatedly for doing less than a complete job, they rarely have undergone voluntary reform.

What this all amounts to is the fact that the institution of education is in turmoil, and that out of that turmoil there may come some change. The leaders of that institution have realized, fairly recently, that they have an obligation to prepare the disadvantaged child for dealing with life. They have come more and more to the conclusion that the best way to do this is through early childhood, or pre-school, education. And they have suddenly found that the institution of education itself is as unprepared for its new task as the disadvantaged child is prepared for dealing with life.

11. Martin Deutsch, "Social and Psychological Perspectives on the Development of the Disadvantaged Learner," *op. cit.*, pp. 236-237.

21

The educational system has its own list of "stimulus deprivations" and "environmental disadvantages" that must be acknowledged, isolated, and corrected if the system hopes to do more than a halfway job of saving the disadvantaged child. And one of the major dangers involved in accepting the philosophy of pre-school education, according to Dr. Deutsch and his colleagues, is that educators will try to provide answers to the child's dilemmas without acknowledging the necessity of solving their own.

Fred M. Hechinger, the education editor of *The New York Times*, writing in a recent collection of essays on pre-school education, found it necessary to warn his readers that new attitudes must be accepted before the educational system may enjoy optimism. He wrote:

> It is exactly because the social crisis and the potential of pre-school education are so real—the one pressing and the other promising—that the danger of turning a new trend into a fad must be recognized and averted.
>
> The search for solutions—a way out of the slums and an answer to the just demands of the civil rights leadership—is frantic. On the success of any action now taken depends a great deal, not least of all social peace in a society which, at least in the crowded urban centers, is on the brink of disastrous warfare. The pre-school experiment sounds so logical and so promising that it has begun to appear to some of those embroiled in the political and educational battle as a magic escape hatch.
>
> Unfortunately, the history of education is paved with good intentions that have led to failure. Those who know the limitations of people as well as of educational methods are well aware that no miracle can assure easy success.
>
> Yet, there are danger signs that the pre-school venture will, by some naive or opportunistic persons, be treated as patent medicine—oversold as a sure cure, followed by the fatal letdown of disappointment.[12]

But the job must be done. It must be done with pretty much the tools that are on hand—the same school boards, administrators, teachers, students, budgets, taxpayers, politi-

---

12. Fred M. Hechinger (editor), *Pre-School Education Today: New Approaches to Teaching Three-, Four-, and Five-Year-Olds*, New York: Doubleday (1966), p. 9.

cians and parents that are involved right now in running the country's educational systems. It must be done quickly, without needless delay, for the longer the nation waits, the more children will be lost. But it also must be done cautiously and without undue emphasis on speed, for false conclusions may be permanently harmful to the children that are involved.

There are many names, and quite a few euphemisms, for what must be done. It has been called early childhood education, early childhood enrichment, pre-school enrichment, and pre-school education. The name that seems to be favored most by the scientists at the Institute for Developmental Studies is *intervention*—a massive intervention, on the part of society, early in the life of the disadvantaged child. It is a strong, simple, clear-cut word that implies, ever so faintly, the idea of an *aggressive* intervention, not only in the lives of the children themselves, but also an aggressive intervention in the way the educational system is being run, and, eventually, in the entire body of relationships between the "larger society" and its disadvantaged members whom it has managed to ignore for so long.

Intervention

As a society, we have arrived at a largely political decision, based on certain objective social conditions, to massively intervene in the development of the child.—Martin Deutsch, in "Social Intervention and the Malleability of the Child," a lecture given at Cornell University in 1965.

Intervention does not mean taking a baby away from its mother, although it does mean sending the child to school at a very early age. It does not mean radically changing the physical environment or even the curriculum of the school, although it does mean making some important revisions. It does not mean supplanting the school teacher with a battery of computers, although it does mean that research has come up with some extremely valuable and somewhat impressive teaching machines, including a typewriter that talks to the child and doesn't allow him to make mistakes.

Intervention does not mean that one agency of society, the schoolroom, is taking over the normal functions and responsibilities of the family, although there is some of that, too. Intervention means taking the disadvantaged child into the classroom early in his life, perhaps at the age of three or four, at the time when he is deemed to be most malleable, and analyzing what his deficiencies are, and then trying to determine how to cope with them.

There are no magic formulae for doing any of this. Martin Deutsch, in his frequent speaking appearances before interested groups of educators, parents, or potential funding sources, is likely to declare, and then to re-emphasize, that "there's no cookbook way of doing this."

There is, of course, a suggested set of curriculum guidelines that is being used by the Institute for Developmental Studies in its experimental classrooms. But the curriculum is constantly undergoing revision and refinement, and an observer of the Institute's work is likely to conclude that to the scientists there, the curriculum itself is not nearly as important as the concepts that are behind it and the people who execute it.

In its published comments on intervention, the Institute has demonstrated consistently this tendency to stay away from specific suggestions, in favor of general conceptions. Says Deutsch:

The task of a compensatory or an enrichment program, as I see it, is

24

to diagnose the deficits and attempt to determine the kinds of programs that will ameliorate them....It becomes apparent that in some way, the child's developmental level must be ascertained. Then cognitive deficits which may be present can be analyzed, and this would be followed by the devising of compensatory educational procedures to ameliorate them.[13]

This does not mean, says Deutsch,

that what should then be supplied to the child is the missing elements in the form in which they are missing. What it does mean is that if one could identify the absent stimuli, one might be helped to identify the particular functions which were not stimulated and so understand better the source of the deficits in cognitive and learning skills. Then educative procedures consistent with the child's developmental level could be devised.[14]

And in another context, he has written:

The critical question...is whether a child can at least start the educational process by learning the basic skills. In order to accomplish this for children from socially marginal backgrounds, I would say that some kind of antecedent experience that would compensate for the inadequacies within the home and the social structure would be very beneficial and would be likely to help the child to achieve a positive adjustment to the demands of the school....

A good pre-school program would attempt to give the child the antecedent preparations for school that the home, community, and at least relative affluence give to the middle-class child. Such programs could be set up only after intensive training of teachers and staff to work on the problems of communicating with the parents as well as developing methods and techniques for compensating the child for a narrowness of experiential variation. The attempt would be to enrich those developmental areas most functional and operative in the school learning situation, thereby establishing both cognitive and attitudinal continuity between the pre-school and the school years....

The skills referred to here would include, for example, the visual and auditory perception which underlie reading, language skills, spatial and temporal orientation, general information, familiarity with books, toys, games, and the development of a sustained curiosity. In addition, the

13. Martin Deutsch, "Social Intervention and the Malleability of the Child," paper read at the annual School of Education Lecture, Cornell University, 1965, p. 9.
14. *Ibid.*, p. 10.

attempt must be made to engage the child as an active participant in the learning process rather than as a passive recipient of a school experience.[15]

So the school must learn how to prepare itself to provide the disadvantaged child with many, if not all, of the experiences and conceptions that he missed at home, and to provide them in a logical order that is attractive to the child and that he is capable of absorbing. It is the Institute's opinion, too, that the school must prepare to do this very early in the child's life, at ages where few schools have trod before. And whatever the school does, it must do it in the spirit of experimentation, constantly aware of the fact that there is no cookbook approach, and that the early answers might be misleading.

Thus it would seem that the essential ingredients in an early childhood intervention program would be, primarily, general ones; that there would be a good deal of "playing it by ear," and less emphasis on doctrinaire assertions of what "will" and what "won't" work. Essentially what the Institute is prescribing is a school system that is committed to doing something about its disadvantaged children, willing to invest the time and resources in finding out what their deficiencies are, and sharp and adventurous enough to then try to determine what the solutions may be. The school system also must be patient, extremely patient in this era of projected breakthroughs that so often fail to materialize. And the school system must be somewhat courageous, in this era of intense pressure for instant, demonstrable success—pressure that comes from the sources of funds, whether they be the Office of Education, the Office of Economic Opportunity, City Hall, a private foundation, a Congressman who measures the success of such programs in the number of riots that don't

15. Martin Deutsch, "Early School Environment: Its Influence on School Adaptations," in Schreiber (editor), *The School Dropout*, Washington: National Education Association (1964), pp. 96-97.

erupt, or a disgruntled taxpayer who wonders quite legitimately if his money is being wasted in a program that cannot possibly demonstrate its success next week, next month, next summer, or even in the next several years.

These qualities of commitment, adventure, patience, and courage are not qualities that typically come to mind when one is asked to describe any of the more traditionally-inclined, rigidly-placed institutions of our society. They certainly do not typically come to mind when one thinks of the institution of education in the United States. But the scientists at the Institute for Developmental Studies feel very strongly that it is *possible* for these qualities to be absorbed by educators and politicians, just as it is *necessary* that they be adopted if the nation hopes to live up to its Constitution and if the massive waste of human potential is to be halted.

Changing the System

The idea of intervention may mean, to some, intervention with the prospect of making the schools and their children classless, or of destroying the middle-class nature of the schools. One might come easily to the conclusion that, given the Institute's findings that the educational disparity is between lower-class children and the middle-classness of the schools which await them, the researchers' aim is to eradicate middle-classness. This is not the case. Dr. Deutsch has carefully pointed out that the Institute's findings do not necessarily condemn middle-class America, nor do they show that it is *bad* for lower-class children to be taught to aspire to middle-class standards. He has explained:

27

It is important to emphasize that the early training to counteract this process [of frustration that comes from not understanding and not succeeding in school] is not a matter of inculcating middle-class values but, rather, of reinforcing the development of those underlying skills that are operationally appropriate and necessary for both successful and psychologically pleasant school learning experiences. The fact that these skills are almost routinely stimulated in middle-class homes does not mean that in content they are middle-class; e.g., there is nothing fundamentally culturally loaded in a good or poor memory, but it can be awfully important in preparing for an examination.[16]

There is, moreover, every reason to believe that middle-class children would benefit, too, from the experiences of an intervention program. Few observers would argue that all is rosy in suburbia. There is "much in middle-class affluent America," says Deutsch, that "tends to destroy individual identity and tends to alienate young people from any purpose outside the self. ... At times, in middle-class children, the need for status replaces the need for individual accomplishment, thereby fostering an apathy toward substantive intellectual achievement similar to that found in children who have been subject to under-stimulation and discrimination."[17]

Once a rationale for intervention has been established and accepted by those who are in positions to carry out intervention, a single but enormously tricky question remains: How can it be done? Or, even more tricky, how can it be done within the framework of the educational institution, using the same parents and children and teachers and administrators and politicians and budgets?

It is at this point that the ideas of the Institute for Developmental Studies might seem to differ most markedly from the ideas of others interested in the field of early childhood education, for the Institute is plainly on record as believing that

16. *Ibid.*, p. 97.
17. Martin Deutsch, "Social Intervention and the Malleability of the Child, *op. cit.*, p. 5.

intervention *cannot* be accomplished within the framework of education as it is known today. In order to change the child, the institution of education must be changed, too. This single fact would seem to mark the Institute's program as the one both most likely to fail and the one most likely to succeed—most likely to fail because any practical assessment of the situation must include the suggestion that the American system of education is a rigid, inflexible thing, not given to innovation and with a tradition of fighting with those who propose change; most likely to succeed because any practical assessment also must accept the fact that the program most likely to succeed is the one that demands a change in the system.

Martin Deutsch believes that a change in the system *is* possible, although bringing about such a change would be a monumental task. But, he quickly asserts, the price of not undertaking that task would be pretty monumental, too. "In part, I think we already have a 'lost generation' of school children," he said in a recent interview. "The problem is, are we going to have another one? And the whole purpose of the intervention program is to guarantee against this happening again, at least on such a massive basis, and gradually to build up the education and the social science know-how so it won't happen again. A lot of it comes down to attitudes, and teacher training, and the kind of commitment one has, and the problem with the school's being a matriarchy, and the problem of advising people of their rights, and other problems. Many of these people who run the schools have a problem themselves —a problem of second-generation removal from lower-class status themselves, and so there is an animosity that has been built in them towards the children they have to deal with. All these problems have to be coped with."

There is the problem, not at all a simple one, of convincing educators that they have some allies in the behavioral sciences. Deutsch has said that in order to promote integration of the disciplines, "a crucial historical difference between education and psychiatry, sociology, and psychology must be recognized. While the latter have the impetus coming from both their newness and their response to challenge, education has the disadvantage of a long and encumbering history."[18]

Not only is there a historical estrangement between educators and behavioral scientists; there seems also to be a feeling of superior status on the part of many behavioral scientists that makes it difficult for them to work with educators. With the exception of those scientists at the Institute for Developmental Studies and similar institutes elsewhere in the nation, there appear to be relatively few psychologists, psychiatrists, and sociologists who actively want to combine their talents with those of the educators. They are willing to measure the work already done by the educators, and they seem eager to pursue organizational studies of the educational institution, but relatively little is being done that is of a truly interdisciplinary nature.

Another problem that must be considered and dealt with before an intervention program may be begun is the problem of retraining teachers (Deutsch uses the term "sensitizing" to refer to the job that must be done with teachers and administrators). Deutsch's colleague, Richard R. Ellis, of the Institute, whose background is educational rather than psychological, reported in a recent paper:

Today there appears to be less patent resistance to ideas of providing educational experiences to young children. The U.S. Federal government is making available hundreds of thousands of dollars for pre-school children in communities all across the nation. Nursery school educators enjoy more visibility now than ever before. But all of this does not mean

18. Martin Deutsch, "Social and Psychological Perspectives on the Development of the Disadvantaged Learner," *op. cit.*, p. 234.

that today there is massive acceptance of educational programming for pre-school children. There is, unfortunately, considerable resistance to this notion by many educators.

We suggest that the differences between the pros and the cons exist partially because of the differing philosophies about fostering development of children, but, partially, also because of the lack of a common understanding of the terminology used.

Traditionally, said Ellis, the philosophy on which nursery schools in the United States have been founded comes from Rousseau. The idea is that the child's development is "an unfolding process," he said, and the proper role of the teacher is to provide warmth and affection and to more or less stay out of the way of the child's development. For most children from advantaged background, this formula works out well:

And well it should: The advantaged child lives in an environment rich in varieties of experiences; available to the child are adults who have had enriched experiences and who wish to share them with the child; a large amount of stimulation and teaching of the child continues from the time he is born—a continuous situation that is tutorial in nature; both teachers and parents hold the same expectations of the child; the culture of the child is continuous with and contiguous to the culture of the school. The advantaged child brings with him to his first day of school a wide range of basic knowledge and skills.

Teachers who see themselves as guardians of the child's natural unfolding tend to see threat to the unfolding process when such words as *structure, organize,* or even *teach* are directed toward their classrooms. Structure could be equated with rigidity, imposed direction, and unrelated intervention. Structure could also mean a flexible framework, a support, a guide, and a goal. To organize could be to disregard individual and group differences of the moment in favor of a prepared plan. To organize could also be to define long-range and short-term goals for individuals and the group; to define the task; to analyze learning; to prepare. To teach could be to operate as a conveyor of content with little regard for learning processes or interests of the learner. To teach could also be to accept responsibility for providing to each learner the best possible learning experiences based on his antecedent learning. Structuring, organizing and teaching are rather global terms, but their meaning becomes important and perhaps more clear as we plan for young disadvantaged children.[19]

Not only must teachers be exposed to new ideas, but the training institutions that provide future teachers must be changed, too, in the view of the Institute. In a document filed with the Office of Economic Opportunity in 1966, the Institute explained why it had found it necessary to set up its own training program for teachers who staffed its demonstration classes:

The Institute recognized that teacher training institutions do not now have the facilities or trained personnel to prepare teachers and related school personnel for the kinds of reality situations and experiences they will meet in teaching the disadvantaged child. The inadequacy of such training programs became clearly visible as antipoverty programs were implemented, and funds released for the establishment of Head Start and community action programs.[20]

There are further dangers associated with planning and starting an intervention curriculum. One of them, the one the Institute fears most, has been expressed by Dr. Deutsch this way:

There seems to be a great need in mid-Twentieth-Century America thoroughly to discuss all problems, investigate their causes, delineate possible solutions, and implement only those solutions that have been sufficiently skeletonized so that they no longer represent threats to the *status quo*. The danger to the approaches discussed here is that it will be put into the context of the stress-free, quasi-"purposeful" play, psychologically supportive, momistically oriented, de-intellectualized, sterile enclosures where much of early childhood education is located. If such takes place, social experimentations in this area could have the fate previously indicated. But if the social scientists and educators undertake such a project jointly in a spirit of experimentation and with

19. Richard Ellis, "Educational Programming for Pre-school Children," speech published in *Child Study* (the bulletin of the Institute for Child Study), Vol. 28, No. 2 (109), (Summer 1966), pp. 24-32 (p. 26).

20. Institute for Developmental Studies, "Progress Report, April 29, 1965-June 30, 1966, and Continuation Proposal, June 1, 1966-June 30, 1967, for Regional Research and Resource Center in Early Childhood," submitted to the Office of Economic Opportunity, March, 1966, pp. 130-131.

joint determination to kill the accumulated sacred cows, the possibilities of success are greatly enhanced.[21]

Among the dangers, too, is the possibility that those in charge of formulating early childhood intervention programs will assume that once a child passes a certain age—say five or six, seven or eight—he will be out of the program's reach. The Institute has found no evidence to back up this idea; indeed, much of its research points toward a continuation of enrichment and intervention through as many pre-kindergarten, kindergarten, and elementary school grades as is possible.

Deutsch also has deplored the idea that "any intervention program is better than none." It is possible, he has said, that negative attitudes can be built into children by sloppy, poorly-put together programs. "A good case can be made for saying that any program which gets the child into a classroom and handling and becoming familiar with school-related materials will have a positive effect on his general attitudes and his comfort in the school situation," says Deutsch. "But this argument too often is used as a rationale for providing a third of a loaf when a rich society has already stolen five loaves from the heritage of many minority group children, and the return of at least one whole one is necessary to obtain any meaningful enhancement of performance."[22]

Deutsch and the Institute have cautioned against the blind acceptance of other assumptions which may be out-and-out dangerous and which, at the very least, deserve examination by anyone attempting to set up an intervention program:

1. "... that for a limited period of time, if a rich, structured program is begun for children when they are three or four years of age, it will ignite growth potential which had up un-

21. Martin Deutsch, "Early School Environment: Its Influence on School Adaptation," *op. cit.*, p. 100.
22. Martin Deutsch, "Social Intervention and the Malleability of the Child," *op. cit.*, p. 7.

til then been dormant in the child." Another way of putting this, writes Deutsch, is to say that "a deprived early environment simply prevents the normal cognitive development processes from beginning and that a powerful stimulus will kick it off, and that the process will create its own momentum independent of continued expanded environmental stimulation."[23] The studies that have been made of the long-term effects of intervention do not discount this notion, he says, but neither do they support it.

2. That the curriculum, as it is being revised to meet the needs of lower-class children, must be downgraded in the process. "That is exactly what has to be avoided," Deutsch has written, "if we are to take children from these environments and help them to develop to a point where they will be eligible for the kind of job training that will be required in the future. There may have to be a modification—and perhaps serious modification—of the curriculum at various levels."[24]

3. That "when there has been limitation of environmental encounters the child should be exposed to as much compensatory stimulation as possible. The assumption is that there is a limited period of time for the acceleration of cognitive development because of the presumed hypothetical period during which the child is said to be optimally receptive...."

A parallel assumption here is that the experiences which a child missed earlier in his life can be pumped into his brain later on, and that the compensation thus may be accomplished with ease. "Programs which simply provide the overall experiences which a child has missed at an earlier age," writes Deutsch, "may well be ineffective. The experience which must be provided is that which will stimulate the growth of the

23. *Ibid.*, p. 7.
24. Martin Deutsch, "Some Elements in Compensatory Education," the text of a talk given in Sausalito, California, p. 4.

desired skill at the child's current level of development, age, socialization, etc. Experiences missed cannot be retrieved. What probably can be retrieved, however, is the development that would have been stimulated by the missed experiences had they been present. But that development at a later time must be stimulated by experiences consistent with the later, rather than the earlier, time."[25]

One example of a false application of this assumption is the first-grade teacher who takes her lower-class children on a field trip to the zoo—a place with which middle-class first graders are quite familiar, but which the poorer children may be seeing for the first time. Deutsch's argument, which will be amplified later, is that the teacher should not just take the children to the zoo and expect them to absorb, at six years of age, and in one afternoon, all the concepts they would have brought with them to the zoo if they had been middle-class— the concepts of size, color, furriness, categories of animals, and so forth. Rather the teacher must structure the visit to the zoo, and the days before and after the trip, to make certain that the proper concepts are introduced at the proper time and in the proper sequences.

Deficits

It is the Institute's contention that timing is of extreme importance throughout the planning, initiation and operation of any intervention program. Writes Deutsch:

It is in the transitional years from the pre-school period through the elementary school years that the child is first subject to the influence

25. Martin Deutsch, "Social Intervention and the Malleability of the Child," *op. cit.*, pp. 7-9.

and the requirements of the broader culture. It is then that two environments are always present for him: the home environment and the school environment. But it is also in these transitional—and especially pre-transitional—years that the young organism is most malleable. Thus, it is at that point that efforts might best be initiated to provide a third—an intervention—environment to aid in the reconciliation of the first two. Such reconciliation is required because, especially for the child from a disadvantaged background, there are wide discrepancies between the home and school milieus. In the intervention environment, preventative and remedial measures can be applied to eliminate or overcome the negative effects of the discontinuities....

Apparently, it is not sufficient to provide particular stimulation for the growing individual, but it must be supplied at a special time, or within particular time limits, if it is to have the most desired effect.... There are insufficient data to hypothesize a most critical period for learning in the human child, and there are probably different critical or optimal periods for different functions. However, at about three or four years of age there is a period which would roughly coincide with the early part of which Piaget calls the 'preoperational stage.' It is then that the child is going through the later stages of early socialization; that it is required that he focus his attention and monitor auditory and visual stimuli; and that he learn through language to handle simple symbolic representations. It is at this three-to-four-year-old level that organized and systematic stimulation through a structured and articulated learning program might most successfully prepare the child for the more formal and demanding structure of the school. It is here at this early age that we can postulate that compensation for prior deprivation can most meaningfully be introduced, and, most important, there is considerably less that has to be compensated for at this age than exists when a far more complex and at least somewhat less plastic child gets to the first grade.[26]

The educator who is searching for the best age at which to start an intervention program must also face the prospect of deciding when the program will end. Of course, one answer to this may well be "When the money stops coming in." There is a limit on the supply of money to be invested in interven-

26. Martin Deutsch, "Social and Psychological Perspectives on the Development of the Disadvantaged Learner," *op. cit.*, pp. 238-239.

tion programs. And such programs could be, and should be, expensive—far more expensive than the present cost of maintaining the *status quo*. Deutsch has suggested that an intervention program should spend a minimum of $1,200 per student for each academic year, not allowing for inflation. Expenditures of this magnitude might be considered ordinary by superintendents of the more wealthy suburban school systems, but they would represent quite a jump for systems in the decaying urban centers.

Much, undoubtedly most, and very close to all of the experimentation that is being done now in early childhood education is being funded by Washington, which has reiterated its intention not to slacken the war on poverty and ignorance. Some critics remain concerned, though, that the lack of smashing, flashy victories in early childhood education may tempt the funding sources to look elsewhere for recipients who promise to deliver quick results.

If it could be assumed, though, that the money will continue coming in, the question of the length of an intervention program must be considered. The Institute's own demonstration classes in the New York City school system run now through the third grade. Deutsch has argued that "to assure stability of programs, it would be desirable to continue special programs for several more years...it would seem that the child from the pre-school and enriched kindergarten classes might best remain in a special ungraded sequence through the third-grade level, a period in which he could be saturated with basic skill training and not be allowed to move on until he has attained basic competence in the skills required by the higher grades."[27] Of course, an important side effect of the teacher retraining advocated by the Institute would be to equip instructors at all levels—from pre-kinder-

---

27. *Ibid.*, pp. 242-243.

garten through high school—with the skills and sensitivities that are necessary for the education of disadvantaged children.

On the subject of teacher-pupil ratios, the Institute's findings are not surprising. A good ratio for pre-kindergarten classes, experience has shown, is seventeen students to two teachers—one of the teachers being a "head teacher," and the other being her assistant.

The Institute is cautious about starting an intervention program that is too big. "We believe it is much better," writes Deutsch, "to have fewer classes that are fully equipped and operated in the best way we now know than to increase the number and do a halfway job with more children." And a school system must be careful in the techniques it uses to select the children for an intervention program. "A problem encountered in the attempt to select the most disadvantaged children," says the director, "is the tendency of the more aware and upwardly mobile parents—those who are best able themselves to prepare their children for school—to find out about preschool programs and to apply for admittance."[28]

The most important consideration, of course, is that which determines the actual components of an intervention program—the curriculum itself. But the Institute for Developmental Studies would not even at this point wish to embark on a discussion of what constitutes a proper curriculum. Before that can be attempted, the Institute would argue, even more homework must be done.

For one thing, the educator must determine what the deficits are that lower-class children might bring to his particular intervention program.It is not enough to assume that the poorer children are just "behind" their middle-class contemporaries in reading and language and familiarity with the

28. Martin Deutsch, "What We've Learned About Disadvantaged Children," *op. cit.*, pp. 50-51.

alphabet. Much of the Institute's work has been in attempting to isolate the difficulties of these children and to determine what caused them in the first place; only after they are isolated and analyzed does the Institute attempt to construct programs to ameliorate them.

From its own work and out of its research and the research of others, the Institute has developed two hypotheses which, the Institute feels, are essential in the planning and execution of any specific program. One is called the "Cumulative Deficit Hypothesis."[29] It states that "children from socially disadvantaged environments, without the benefit of an intervening enrichment program, will consistently lose ground as they progress in school. In relationship to their more advantaged peers, these children show a progressive loss in varied test scores."

The other hypothesis is that "there are specific features of the lower-class environment, as assessed by the Institute's 'Deprivation Index,' which, if not therapeutically assuaged, have a deleterious effect on the development of abilities related to academic success."

The longer these "specific negative environmental factors" exist, says the Institute, "the greater is the deficit associated with them." And, further, the diminution of these factors "may be associated with improvement in school and general cognitive functioning, even in children of low socioeconomic status."[30]

What the Institute is saying, then, is that it believes "deprivation" may be made up of several components; that those components must be recognized and dealt with methodically if an enrichment or intervention program is to succeed. The

29. Benjamin Bloom discusses this concept in his book, *Stability and Change in Human Characteristics*, New York: John Wiley, (1964).
30. Institute for Developmental Studies, "Progress Report...", *op. cit.*

Institute constructed a "Deprivation Index," consisting of six variables which were combined into a composite score, and tried out the index on samples of New York school children, black and white.

The variables include the degree of dilapidation of the child's home (taken from Census data); the parents' aspirations for a child's educational level; the number of children under the age of eighteen in the home; the degree of conversation at the dinner table; the number of cultural experiences anticipated by the child for the coming weekend; and, the attendance or non-attendance of the child at a kindergarten.

The Deprivation Index was used on children who also had taken standard intelligence tests. The Institute reported:

> The results indicate that the Deprivation Index tends to act as a factor independent of socioeconomic status and race in contributing to variations in test performance. Thus significant main effects on both tests were related to the Deprivation Index even in groups homogeneous with respect to race or socioeconomic status. This suggests that cumulations of specific environmental factors (e.g., low parental motivation, absence of kindergarten experience) can have a disadvantaging effect despite relatively high socioeconomic status, and that the diminution of such features may have an advantageous effect despite relatively low socioeconomic status. This latter point provides support for enrichment programs aimed at alleviating the effects of social disadvantage on children of lower socioeconomic status...we see that decrements in test performance associated with Negro or lower-class status tend to be offset or mitigated in the context of cumulations of specific, advantaging environmental factors.[31]

Proceeding from the idea that if the specific negative environmental factors can be diminished, the child will benefit, the Institute has directed its research at determining just what those specific factors are. The results have been placed

31. *Ibid.*

into four categories, each of which should not be thought of as a separate and distinct classification, but which, with a great deal of overlapping, help to explain what a child's weaknesses are and point to the direction educators and behavioral scientists may search in order to alleviate those weaknesses. The categories are language, conceptual abilities, reading, and self-concept and social interaction.

Some of the specific weaknesses that fit into one or more of the four categories may be recognized immediately; others are more obscure. There is great emphasis at the Institute on acknowledging that one weakness may be quite dependent and overlapping on one or more others, and that it is somewhat dangerous to try to categorize them too much. Frequently the Institute, when commenting on the four categories, will emphasize that they have been categorized only to facilitate discussion.

Some of the Institute's findings in each of the categories have been described this way:

In *language*, the problems that have been identified include "a general lack of continuity in communication of information between the home and school, and, in particular, between the disadvantaged child and the teacher"; a widespread lack of knowledge, on the part of researchers, about what periods of the child's life are best suited for language training; and the lack of conclusive study on the differences that exist in the speech patterns between lower- and middle-class children.

In *conceptual abilities*, the Institute has found that the lower-class child has greater difficulties with abstraction than does the middle-class child. He tends to function on the concrete level. And standardized tests that can adequately mea-

41

sure the slum child's concept formation are yet to be developed (although the Institute is working on them).[32]

In *reading*, it has been determined that the lower-class child has difficulties not only with his reading skills, but also—and more importantly—with the skills that underlie reading skills. Because his abilities to discriminate visually and auditorily are less developed than those of middle-class children, he has more difficulty with reading. And because his language ability is less advanced, he suffers there, too.

In *self-concept* and *social interaction*, the Institute and others have found ample evidence that the lower-class children tend more than other children to have negative self concepts. The negative images of himself that are brought by the child from his home in the slum or the all-black ghetto, Deutsch says, are amplified and reinforced in the classroom

32. Lassar G. Gotkin and other members of the Institute staff have offered one definition of "conceptual abilities" in their pamphlet, "Research in the Acquisition of Pre-Reading Skills Using a 'Talking Typewriter,' " a publication prepared for distribution among educators and others who are about to visit the Institute's demonstration programs. The conceptual skills, they say, primarily "are concerned with responding correctly to the ways in which the elements of written and spoken language are organized and coordinated. The concept of order is a particularly important skill, since all language is ordered. Written language is ordered from left to right, and spoken language is ordered in time. The child must acquire numerous concepts related to order: With written language he must recognize that 'ton,' 'not' and 'otn' must be responded to differently—while the child might *see* these as different-looking groups, he may still *treat* them as being the same because they all include the same letter-shapes. Thus, he would have the *perceptual* skill, that is, seeing that the letter-shapes were not identical in appearance because the elements were ordered differently. However, he would lack the conceptual skill of order, that is, the realization that the ordering of the elements is important to differentiating the sequence from one another. There are many other conceptual skills. In the auditory realm, an important skill is the ability of a child to attend to and identify the initial sound in spoken (and, later, printed) words. Notice that this skill requires attention to the *first* sound, so that the child must have had some previous experience with the skill of order to solve this problem. Another example of a conceptual pre-reading skill is the concept that the smallest units of written language, letters, can be organized into larger units by means of spaces between sequences of letters. Possession of this concept in turn facilitates the ability of the child to perceive such a *sequence* of letters as a discrete unit in itself, rather than as a series of smaller discrete units. In a mature reader, this skill is refined, unified, automatic, and almost unconscious. Mastery of this skill quite likely lays the groundwork for the development of much more complex reading skills in which the units become much larger: phrases, even whole sentences."

by "the frustration inherent in not understanding, not succeeding, and not being stimulated in the school, while being regulated by it....Horizons and goals are stimulated early in life, and if the parents have had low ceilings in terms of variety of experiences, with the intensity being in terms of job insecurity, negotiations with welfare and landlords, and the like, there is not much left to give the child a sense of identifying the self with goals that take individual impetus and disciplining."[33]

Building a Curriculum

Taking the specific negative characteristics into consideration, the Institute has proceeded to build a curriculum around them. "It is our hypothesis," said the Institute in its 1966 progress report to the Office of Economic Opportunity, "that the disadvantaged child needs a specially sequenced curriculum, designed to build cognitive skills and improve linguistic and perceptual abilities. This curriculum should be continued through at least the first three school years in addition to the two pre-school years if the disadvantaged child is to develop the more logical and abstract thought processes needed for learning and academic success. The Institute has been developing a sequenced curriculum which emphasizes the development of a positive self-concept and a high motivation level."[34]

The program is further built on the idea that the child's

33. Martin Deutsch, "Early Social Environment: Its Influence on School Adaptation," *op. cit.*, pp. 97-98.
34. Institute for Developmental Studies, "Progress Report...", *op. cit.*, p. 86.

own sequence of learning is threefold: from sensory-motor to perceptual to conceptual. Richard Ellis has explained the three stages in this fashion:

Another assumption is that a given aspect of the environment exerts a different influence on development of a function at different times. There are probably certain kinds of stimuli that provide more advantage to development of a function.

We assume, borrowing from Piaget, that in learning there is a developmental progression, a sequence including three stages or levels of learning and development: 1) The sensory-motor level, in which perceptual discriminations are facilitated through the child's actual contact with materials, and learning the correct labeling and mediational responses; 2) The perceptual level, in which discriminations are facilitated through the presentations of contrasting stimuli (different colors, shapes, sizes, and sounds) and their coordination with differentiated verbal levels; and 3) The ideational-representational level, in which situations are presented through verbal and conceptual levels with a minimum of concrete perceptual support.[35]

Ellis offers as examples of the three levels the act of riding a bicycle, which is learned through motor response; the realization that "images stand for events," which would illustrate the perceptual level; and the "ability to use natural or formal language," a demonstration of the conceptual, or ideational-representational level.[36]

Not only should the sequence of a curriculum be considered vital by anyone attempting to start an intervention program, but other ingredients—which the Institute refers to as step size, pacing, and feedback—are important, too. Writes Ellis:

The preferred sequence is from simple to complex, both within an element and from element to element. We could have the child learn to recognize and label one shade of one color, for example, blue, before we would ask him to tell us everything in the room that is blue. A simple sequence in color learning might begin, for example, by giving the child a number of identical objects, all of which are colored the same shade

35. Ellis, *op. cit.*, p. 27.
36. *Ibid.*, p. 27.

of blue. He is told the proper label, and uses this label as he handles the objects. A second set of objects, identical to the first, but of a different, single shade of color is given to the child. Again, he is given the proper label and he handles the objects. The sequence continues by having the child sort a mixture of the two sets into the two classifications of color.

Steps within each sequence must be small enough for the child to cope with. After he has learned to sort correctly two different colors, perhaps he is ready for the introduction of a third color. The total number of objects comprising the three colors, however, might require a reduction if we are not to overwhelm him. What to us might seem to be tiny steps are usually giant strides to the disadvantaged child.

After the child has had several color-learning experiences and several shape-learning experiences, we can ask questions of him commensurate with these experiences. The question, 'Are you holding a blue circle or a yellow circle?' varies only one element, color. Sequentially this question would precede the more complex task presented in, 'Are you holding a blue circle or a yellow rectangle?' Here, both elements vary. Further along the sequence we might ask, 'What are you doing?' Whatever the required response is, it must not be beyond the child's ability.

In another example we might require the child to identify the blue circle from among several stimuli. A lower task level would offer a choice between a blue circle and a single totally different object. Complexity of task increases with the addition of more objects. When more objects are present there can also be an increased need for finer discriminations. An even higher level of task would be to select the blue circle from a variety of rounded shapes, e.g., ellipses or ovals, whose colors are violet, purple, and so on.

Proper pacing allows the child to proceed from element to element at the rate most comfortable for him. As he works his way through a sequence, he may be capable of rapidly devouring some steps, or he may require relatively greater amounts of time with other steps. Pacing is an individual matter, and, if this matter is sacrificed by the teacher for reasons of expediency, then the child might be pushed ahead while 'soft spots' or incomplete notions might remain to plague him. For the disadvantaged child this could be especially disastrous. His environment might not provide him with means to fill in the gaps. It is the teacher's responsibility to insure his learning of basic skills and information at each step of the way.

Feedback, the response from the materials or teacher that gives the child confirming or corrective information, is a vital consideration. Through feedback the child learns which track he is on, which stimuli he should focus upon. He receives reinforcement of prior learning; he receives affirmative or corrective response to his applications of learning. The more immediate the feedback to his response, the more impact on learning can the feedback have.[37]

Feedback, warns Ellis, can present problems in the sort of group situations that prevail in a classroom. If the class responds as a whole to a teacher's question, the teacher may have difficulty recognizing one student's particular individual difficulties. Ellis continues:

The problem is manifest when the teacher responds to the most verbal or loudest children in the group. In responding to these children, she might miss completely a major portion of the children. The problem is compounded when we teach young children, because they are quite limited in the varieties of responses they can offer to a given situation. Feedback problems in group situations suggest that a more individualized approach to the teaching-learning experience may be more profitable for certain kinds of learnings.

The individual child isn't the only one who profits from feedback. He provides feedback to the teacher, and she learns how the child perceives his task, at what level he is operating, at what speed he is moving, and how effective her teaching is.

An issue here is the way in which teachers structure questions. With young children we have found a technique of asking questions to be useful; this technique might be described as using 'dichotomous questions.' That is, the child is given a choice: 'Are you holding a blue circle or a yellow circle?' 'Are you holding a blue circle or a blue rectangle?' Through these questions the teacher limits the problem and provides the language; the child chooses the response.

In other words, the structure of a teacher's question sets the level of the task required of the child. Suppose, for example, that the child is holding a blue circle, and the teacher asks him, 'What are you doing?' The variety of responses possible and correct is enormous. For a four-year-old child correctly to tell her in response to the question that he is holding a blue circle can be a mammoth achievement. He has cate-

37. *Ibid.*, pp. 28-29.

gorized an object simultaneously along two dimensions; he has supplied both labels; and, perhaps even more difficult, he has supplied the proper verb. In her question she required him to select a narrow band from a wide range of possibilities, and to select a specific response from the narrow band. Her question is not much help to him; it is neither dichotomous nor specific. He could wonder if she meant is he sitting or standing; or looking at Joey; or playing a naming game; or holding a paper; and so on.

Perhaps deciding on a response is beyond his ability. The child may not arrive at a decision. And what has the teacher found out? In his wondering the child used a great deal of language, each involving different concepts. But did the teacher's question tap this language? Does she conclude from his non-response that he does not recognize a circle, or the color blue, or that he is holding it?

Ideally, the teacher gives the child varieties of opportunities to demonstrate his knowledge of concepts if she is to know that he knows.

It is easy to say that she should provide varieties of opportunities for the child to demonstrate his knowledge of a concept. This task for the curriculum developer, though, is difficult. To ask a child with a blue circle what he is holding, we must be confident that he has opportunity to learn the concept of blue and the concept of circle. If we employed the dichotomous questions mentioned earlier, we would be presenting to the child a task of a lower order than is inherent in the question, 'What are you holding?' However, we could ask, 'Are you holding a blue circle or a yellow rectangle?'...To provide the child with more variety of opportunity to demonstrate his knowledge of blue circle, we could ask him to select the blue circle from among several different stimuli. The point here is that the structure of the teacher's question can provide varieties of experiences at a given level of task, and the structure of her question can also change drastically the level of the task.[38]

Dr. Ellis' remarks, and similar comments made on this subject by Dr. Deutsch and others at the Institute, should provide some indication of the meticulousness with which the Institute for Developmental Studies approaches the task of constructing a proper curriculum for an early childhood intervention program. It is this sense of detail, which the In-

38. *Ibid.*, pp. 29-30.

47

stitute's own research has shown to be so important, that pervades every bit of the curriculum that now is being planned, executed, and evaluated. It is this idea that the teacher constantly must *go back* in her analysis and perceptions of the child, to determine, through acutely sensitive observation and informal testing, as well as through standardized testing instruments, whether the child has the fundamental information, the information that he must have if he or the teacher, are to be expected to build anything. It is the idea that a child cannot learn the alphabet without first demonstrating that his mind can discriminate between the sharp angles of an "A" and the perfect curve of an "O," and, further (and later), the more relatively subtle difference between the endless curve of an "O" and the interrupted curve of a "C." Thus it is not surprising that a visitor to the Institute's demonstration program, to a pre-kindergarten classroom in Public School 175 in Harlem, will notice two, not one, of the familiar ring-stacking games on a storeroom shelf. This game consists of a round base with a dowel set into it; around the dowel, a child stacks movable rings of wood of decreasing diameter. One of the ring-stacking games in the storeroom of the pre-kindergarten class is of the standard variety, which may be purchased at any toy counter; the rings are painted different, bright colors. But the other one has been altered. The Institute has painted all the rings yellow.

A visitor may ask why. The teacher, Mrs. Vicki Breitbart, replies: "Because it's too difficult for some of the children to cope with two different things at the same time—both color and size. We use the all-yellow rings to teach them the concept of size; when we think they've gotten that, *then* we can move on to the more complicated job of stacking rings that are different in color and size." The Institute calls this "isolation of stimuli."

Nor is it surprising that Mrs. Breitbart and the other teachers who have been trained by the Institute carry this same sort of attention to detail into every corner of their classroom day—this sensitivity about using every available opportunity to confront the disadvantaged children in their classrooms with concepts that will be important to them for the rest of their lives—concepts that middle-class children bring to school with them and concepts that the public school system traditionally has assumed were understood by all beginning first-graders. There is a snack time in the pre-kindergarten classroom at P.S. 175; one reason for it is that the school authorities realize that many of the children do not receive the proper nourishment at home. But the Institute has seen to it that even snack time is educational; the children use different sorts of cereal to learn the concepts of shape (including the shape of letters of the alphabet; one of the cereals *is* made up of alphabet-shaped pieces); they calculate the relative length of straws; they talk about the comparative sweetness of cereal with sugar and cereal without sugar. "They cognitively eat," explained one Institute official with a smile. The process is constant, as a look at one day in Mrs. Breitbart's classroom will indicate.

A Day in a Classroom

Mrs. Breitbart and her assistant teacher, Miss Jill Jacobson, had been in the classroom since 8:15 A.M. They had carefully put together a toy barn, with fences and miniature farm animals, in the top of a cardboard carton, and they had put about half an inch of dirt into the carton. Both teachers agreed that they didn't have the slightest idea how the little farm was going to be received by the students.

49

At 8:45 A.M., the children started to arrive. There were seventeen children in the pre-kindergarten class. All of them were Negroes, and all of them were past the age of four; they would be eligible to go to the public school system's kindergarten in the 1967-68 school year.

Mrs. Breitbart is a 1963 graduate of Sarah Lawrence. "Most of my courses were in art and literature," she said one day. "There was no thought of teaching. But in my last year at Sarah Lawrence, I took an excellent psychology course, and we worked in the nursery school that Sarah Lawrence runs. That got me interested." A friend told her about the Institute, and Mrs. Breitbart joined as an assistant teacher in September of 1963. At the same time, she started taking the education courses necessary for her to obtain her teaching license. She became a head teacher for the Institute in the academic year 1965-66. Miss Jacobson, who studied anthropolgy and sociology at Wellesley, was in her first year of serving as an assistant teacher.

"Good morning. Good morning. Hello, Raleigh. Good morning, Deborah. Good morning, Earl. Good morning, Craig. How are you? Fine!"[39] Mrs. Breitbart was careful to welcome each child by name (for many of them, there had been few occasions when someone referred to them by name). Along one wall of the room was a row of child-sized wooden lockers. On the door of each locker was a child's name, and below the name was a small photograph of the child. There was a large mirror in one corner of the room, where the children could see them-

39. Because it seemed that one way to explain the work of the Institute for Developmental Studies would be to provide examples of the teachers' actual classroom work, a transcript of a day in the pre-kindergarten classroom was obtained during the winter of 1966-67. The teacher wore a microphone and a tiny electronic transmitter, which broadcast her words and most of the children's replies, without connecting wires, to a receiver and a tape recorder that were situated in an out-of-the-way part of the room. Inquisitive children were told immediately the purpose of the electronic equipment, and no attempt was made to hide it. The presence of the equipment did not intimidate or inhibit them in any noticeable way.

selves, full length, probably for the first times in their lives.

The classroom seemed brighter and more cheerful than most New York City school system classrooms. One reason for this, undoubtedly, was the relative newness of the school building. But there was something else, something not immediately apparent. To one visitor, it looked as if the classroom had been laid out so that it might serve its students better, not arranged for the benefit of the teachers or arranged to make discipline easier to impose.

Nowhere in the composition of the room, in the chairs, tables, shelves, or toys, was there an indication of rigid *group* work—a situation in which all the children would sit passively in front of the teacher.[40] The materials and furniture in the room were arranged, rather, to give the distinct impression of the uniqueness of each piece of furniture, each toy; a number of areas where children with individual interests might find entertainment and knowledge. And as the children filed into the room, they gravitated quickly to the places that interested them most, and the teachers gravitated to the chil-

40. The classroom did not just happen to be different. A lot of the Institute's time has gone into planning the physical and intellectual layout of the rooms. Miss Edwina Meyers, an Institute training instructor, told a group of visitors to the program once that "Our classrooms are based on traditional procedures, *plus.*" And Mrs. Laura Schneider, Institute curriculum supervisor for the pre-kindergarten classes, added: "We use basically the nursery school day. We provide more structure and organization than the traditional nursery school; more focus on the cognitive skills. We're trying to move away from the middle-class focus on emotional development."

An Institute document comments further: "The disadvantaged child must be assisted in terms of the broader society that he must enter. The situation to which society has best access in order to accomplish this is the classroom itself—its physical arrangement, the number and kinds of materials available, and the teacher's attitude toward the children and the materials. The enrichment classrooms have retained the best physical features of a good nursery classroom and have added equipment necessary to stimulate a stimulus-deprived population. The emphasis has been placed on the *use* of these materials in a *relevant* way—relevant to the issue at hand and also to broader knowledge about learning and development in early childhood.

"The enrichment classroom is physically arranged to build the child's concepts of order and space. A perceptually clear and distinct room environment is created

dren, speaking to each of them, giving them individual attention.

A door led directly from the classroom to a lavatory for the children. There were two large tables that would accommodate all of the students. Along one wall was a working surface made of hard plastic. In it were two sinks, both at child height. One of the sinks stood in what the teachers called the "slop corner," the place where children may play with paints, dirt, flour, water, and similar materials.

Child-sized shelves and bookcases were used to define three rectangular areas of the room, the library, and the miniature kitchen, and the area where blocks and heavier toys were stored. A central piece of furniture was a set of movable stairs—three wooden steps going up, and three wooden steps going down. Near the entrance to the classroom were a table and a chair and reading material for visiting parents. On the table there were copies of *Story of the Negro*, by Arna Bontemps; *Go Tell it on the Mountain*, by James Baldwin; *Strength to Love*, by the Rev. Dr. Martin Luther King Jr., and issues of *Ebony* and *Woman's Day*. One piece of furniture was missing: It was the teacher's desk. There was little need for a teacher's desk, because the teachers were constantly on the move, giving the children individual attention.

"I've got a new hat," said one of the children.

"You went shopping with Mommy?" said Mrs. Breitbart.

---

by uncluttered equipment and furniture arranged in an orderly fashion. This arrangement is expected to help the child focus his attention on the curriculum. instead of being distracted by irrelevant stimuli in the classroom. It should be stressed that pressures are not exerted on any child to keep the room orderly. Rather, daily contact with an uncluttered environment is believed helpful in teaching time and space organization. Tidiness is only a secondary benefit....Another result is expected from the structural simplicity of the classroom. Skill in dealing with routines and arrangement, combined with a growing acquisition of skills in other areas, are expected to help a child feel competent in the learning situation. With continued motivation toward learning, the child can then focus more successfully on the cognitive and creative aspects of the curriculum." (Institute for Developmental Studies, "Annual Report 1965," *op. cit.*, p. 59.)

An intervention curriculum contains most of the same basic elements that might be found in any public school classroom. What is impressive about intervention is that those basic elements are used differently. Children in the Institute for Developmental Studies' experimental classrooms still are encouraged to join the free-expression school of painting . . .

... and they still are invited to put pencil to paper ...

. . . and to contemplate the mysteries of nature . . .

. . . and to read . . .

But each activity in the Institute classroom, whether it is taking one's coat off in the morning or eating snacks in mid-day, is associated with one or more of the four areas that the Institute feels is important: language, conceptual abilities, reading, and self-concept and social interaction.

"They cognitively eat," said one Institute official with a laugh . . .

. . . and familiarity with books is considered more important at the younger grades than the ability to recite a book's contents by rote . . .

The children constantly are being called on to weigh, estimate, measure, to learn the importance of comparison and relativity . . .

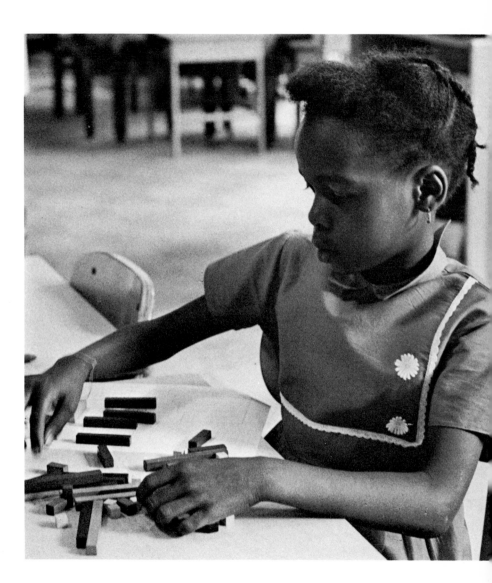

. . . and to discover such concepts as texture . . .

. . . and to sort things out . . .

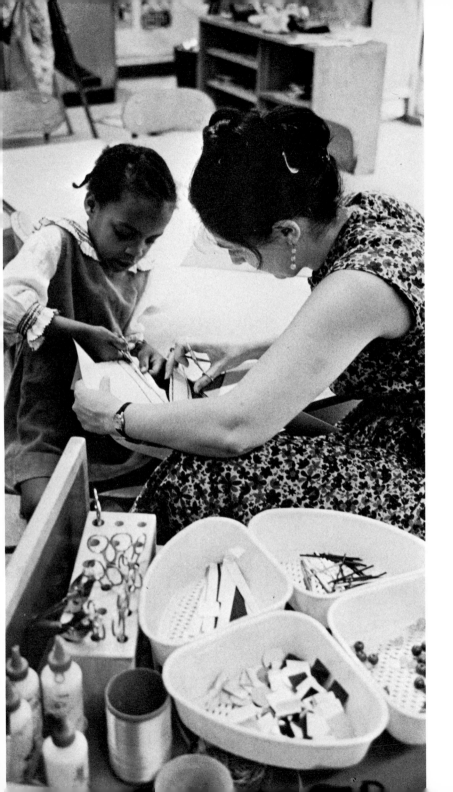

. . . and to build and imagine . . .

. . . and to explore the mechanics of the modern world . . .

. . . and to consider the people who populate the world . . .

The classrooms reflect the Institute's emphasis on individual attention. The various areas of interest are simple, neat, and relatively uncluttered. But most important, they are laid out to serve the students rather than the teacher.

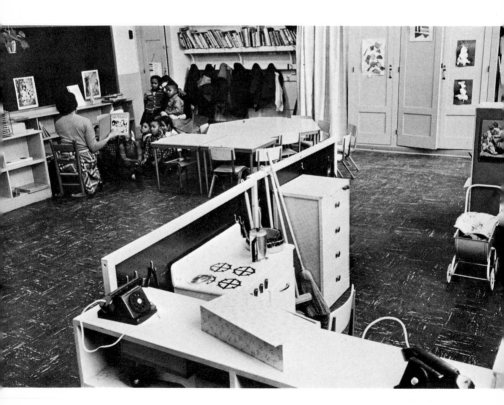

The children's names are prominent in an enrichment classroom. The Institute's researchers think that disadvantaged children, with their particular problems of self-esteem, will benefit from repeated and proud use of their names. Names are posted on their individual lockers . . .

. . . names identify each child's work . . .

... and name-building by matching letters is used to explore the alphabet ...

It is important, too, that the children see themselves as potential grownups. A child from a poor family needs just as much as a middle-class child to dress up in an adult's hats and high heels . . .

... or to pretend he's an adult ...

. . . or to dance . . .

. . . or to pretend that she's on television . . .

. . . and to have some visual evidence that people who are like him—people whose skins are dark, or people who talk the way he does—can be successful, can attain positions of importance, can escape from the mental ghetto.

Intervention does not mean replacing the teacher with a computer. It does mean using the machinery at hand—machinery as exotic as a typewriter that talks to the child and does not allow him to make mistakes—but it also means relying on the savvy of the good teacher who knows her children's individual needs.

"My Mommy and my Daddy took me," the child replied.

(Later, Mrs. Breitbart said she had been moved by the reply. "If we can just break through with him, I'll feel as if we have accomplished something," she said. "This was the longest sentence he's said this year.")

Mrs. Breitbart and Miss Jacobson moved about the room, welcoming the children and directing them to their lockers and engaging in endless bits of small talk. "This is incidental conversation," said the teacher afterward, "which is very important to them." A child went straight to the toy farm, poked her finger in the dirt, and exclaimed, "A garden!" A little boy went to a shelf and got a large magnet and started picking up nails with it.

Mrs. Breitbart asked William if he had remembered to bring a note from home; he hadn't. But he was proud of a piece of paper he had brought in that had pieces of tile glued to it. His brother had made it. Mrs. Breitbart admired it. She complimented Donald on his new haircut; she talked of Batman with Bobby. She hardly ever failed to call a child by name when she was talking with him.

One little boy said, "I didn't come to school yesterday."

"You know what?" asked the teacher. "Neither did I." "No school was yesterday?" said the child. "Right," said Mrs. Breitbart, and they both laughed.

Franklin walked over to a poster that had an empty paper orange juice carton glued to it, and he pointed to his name. The teachers assign two children each day to the jobs of getting the early-morning juice and, later, getting the milk for the snack. The children's names are displayed on the proper poster. Mrs. Breitbart had forgotten to update the orange juice poster, and Franklin reminded her that his name was on the sign, and he had gotten the juice on the previous school day.

53

Ronald walked in, and Mrs. Breitbart welcomed him. "Today I'll let you make a necklace," she said, "because I found some string. Here's your string, and here's some beads. You have to make a knot at one end. And then you can just sit right over there and do that." Ronald had expressed an interest, on the Friday before, to string a necklace. Mrs. Breitbart remembered to find some string over the weekend.

Bobby went to work with the Tinker Toys. Another child went directly to a set of colored plastic panels and held them in front of his eyes. Earl and William started playing with the magnet. Mrs. Breitbart saw that each child was doing something that appealed to him, and then she announced: "You know, we're going to the zoo tomorrow; the whole class is going to the zoo tomorrow." It was not the first time she had announced the impending trip; she and Miss Jacobson had been preparing the children for it for several days. But, as the teachers explained later, some of the children had very dim ideas of what "next week" and "next Tuesday" meant, and for some of them the expression, "We're going to the zoo tomorrow," was their first knowledge that the trip was really close at hand.

The first half hour of the pre-kindergarten day is called *work* by the teachers, although the children certainly think of it as play. After receiving juice and crackers, or sometimes orange sections and raisins, they are directed toward the classroom's manipulative toys—the magnets, Lego System toys, Tinker Toys, Play-Doh, cookie tins, beads, and wooden triangles, circles, and squares that fit into slots in a board.

Franklin played with the Lego System. Carefully he stacked the interlocking plastic bricks on top of each other. Mrs. Breitbart knelt down beside him. She saw his play as an opportunity to work with Franklin on discriminating between shorter and taller. "Put your finger on there and feel it," she said, and Franklin placed his finger on the top of the taller stack of plastic rectangles. "Right up to the top. That's right. There should be one more. Now, which is the tallest one? Right. Good, Franklin. See, this goes right up to the top. Does this one feel tall to you?"

There was a crash. "Oh, me, my building fell down," said a child who had been playing with blocks. "What are you going to do about it?" asked Mrs. Breitbart. Then she returned to Franklin. "You really know how to work with that," she told him. "You used them all up? Does that one fit up there? Now, Franklin, which one is the tallest one? Which one's taller, this one or that one? That's right....Now which one is the tallest of all of these? Is that the tallest of all of them? Put it in and see. Does that come up to the top? Okay, we have to decide which one is the tallest now. Is that one right? Is that the tallest one? Very good. Very good."

A child was picking up nails with a magnet. Mrs. Breitbart asked the child how many nails she thought the magnet would lift. "A hundred, maybe?" She steered Bobby over to the Letter Form Board, the device developed by the Institute which consists of three-inch-high wooden alphabet letters that fit into slots on a board. It is practically impossible for a child to misplace one of the letters."[41] In the pre-kindergarten classroom, only the letters "A" through "G" are visible to the children. Mrs. Breitbart had covered up the remaining letters

41. Reported Lassar G. Gotkin and Fairfid Caudle, of the Institute, in a paper titled "The Alphabet as a Sensori-Motor Experience:" "...for some three decades, the whole-word method of teaching has dominated the instructional scene. As part of this approach, teachers have been instructed to avoid teaching the individual letters of the alphabet. And, for most children from middle-class backgrounds, this has been an acceptable course to follow since so many of these children are well on their way to mastery of the alphabet before entering kindergarten, and teaching the alphabet to them is often unnecessary. On the other hand, however, many children from lower-class backgrounds often enter kindergarten with no notion of what the alphabet is about. In one Harlem school, for example, it was found that two-thirds of the children knew no letters of the alphabet upon entering kindergarten, while in a suburban community, forty per cent of the children could pick

so that the children would not be confused by the enormity of their task. After almost three months of intermittent use of the board, most of the four-year-olds knew how to place "A" through "G" in their correct positions on the board.

The teacher found one small group of children playing with the magnets. She explained why Earl's hammer, which was made of iron, stuck to the magnet, and why another child's wooden mallet did not stick. "Does the magnet stick to wood?" she asked. "Will the magnet pick up this piece of wood?" The children answered, "No."

"Will it pick up *this* piece of wood?" The children replied in the negative again. Then Mrs. Breitbart applied the magnet to some nails. "So," she said, "it picks up the nails because they're made out of iron, too."

She went off to settle a dispute in another corner of the

out the letters when they were named by an adult. The differences between middle-class and lower-class children are not limited to the ability to recognize alphabet letters by name, however.

"Research at the Institute for Developmental Studies has indicated that some of the difficulties in learning to name alphabet letters can be attributed to problems in visually discriminating the sounds which go with the letters. The alphabet is a complex symbol system, and its mastery requires the coordination of a variety of visual and auditory skills. For example, for a child to learn the letter 'M,' he must, on the one hand, be able to discriminate it *visually* from among similarly shaped letters such as 'W.' On the other hand, he must be able to discriminate the sounds of the letter name from the names of other letters which have similar sounds, such as 'N.' Furthermore, he must be able to attach the sound which he hears to the shape which he sees. And, finally, he must grasp the concept that letters are simply a means of 'coding' our spoken language into a written one, and vice versa. A child who experiences difficulty in the discrimination skills mentioned is almost certain to experience difficulty in the other skills."

The paper goes on to say that the Institute developed the Letter Form Board "for the purpose of introducing the alphabet as a sensori-motor experience, rather than as an abstract symbolic system." It was felt that the use of a puzzle-like alphabet would allow the student to familiarize himself with the shapes of letters, "without requiring the child to cope simultaneously with sounds of letters. Furthermore, this familiarization could occur at an earlier age than is possible in formal reading instruction. Later on, when formal reading instruction was begun, presumably a child who had mastered the perceptual problems in visual discrimination using three-dimensional solid letters would find it easier to do the same thing when the letters were printed in two-dimensional form."

Another reason for using three-dimensional letters, said the researchers, was that "solid letters used in a manipulative task provide the child with a richer exroom. One of the children let out a squeal: "It can pick up a piece of wood. Watch!" Mrs. Breitbart hurried back. "It *did* pick up a piece of wood? Show me." The child demonstrated. "Oh," said the teacher. "Because it—" She checked herself in mid-explanation, then said: "*Why* did it pick up that piece of wood?"

"Because the nail was in it!" said a child. "Yes!" cried Mrs. Breitbart. "That's right! Right!"

We're Going to the Zoo

About half an hour after the beginning of the school day, Mrs. Breitbart and Miss Jacobson called the children to the

---

perience than that which can be had with two-dimensional letters. By a 'richer' experience is meant an experience in which the child can make use of more than one sense modality, touch as well as vision. A third reason for the design of the Letter Form Board as a task in which letters, in addition to merely being handled, are placed inside letter-shaped slots, is that such a task provides the child with corrective 'feedback'; that is, with information about the correctness of his actions. With very few exceptions, each letter can be placed only in its own letter slot, and only when the letter is oriented correctly. It was anticipated that this corrective feature of the Letter Form Board would help the child to learn to pay attention to the details of shape which differentiate letters of the alphabet, such as the 'tail' of the 'Q,' and the lack of one with the 'O.'

"...The existence of these types of perceptual difficulties becomes apparent when watching a letter-naive child playing with the board. It is common for such children to pick up the 'B,' for example, and to attempt to force it into the 'B' slot in a reversed position, a graphic demonstration of a reversal error. Another type of error which illustrates perceptual problems occurs when the child takes an 'O' and actually attempts to put it into the 'D' slot. In the beginning, the children sometimes seem to feel that if they push hard enough, they can make the letter conform to the shape of the slot, which suggests that the children are trying to solve the problem in a primitive way and are not making use of the relevant visual and tactile feedback. The relevance of instruction becomes apparent when, with increased experience, children begin to scan the board visually and are able to select the correct slot immediately, thereby relinquishing the more primitive trial and error behaviors."

Gotkin and Caudle note that, from an instructional point of view, the Letter Form Board may be considered a teaching machine, since it employs immediate feedback, progress in small steps, individual pacing, and careful sequencing. The board also may be used by children independent of the teacher; she may be freed from the job of constantly overseeing its use.

57

circle. Each child got a mat and put it on the floor, in a circle, with the teachers. A certain amount of singing and clapping in the circle corner was necessary to get some of the children to leave their manipulative toys:

"Good morning, good morning, good morning to Bobby," sang Mrs. Breitbart. "Good morning, good morning, good morning to Craig." She sang good morning to Adam, and then Donald, and then she sang: "Good morning, good morning, good morning to—who's that?" She pointed at a child. The other children chorused his name. Mrs. Breitbart did the same with Felicia and Ronald. Then she moved directly from the good morning song to a question.

"You know where we're going tomorrow?" The children cried, "Where?" Mrs. Breitbart replied, "We're going to the zoo," and then she broke into song again.

"We're going to the zoo-oo, yes indeed, yes indeed, yes indeed;

"We're going to the zoo-oo, yes indeed, yes indeed, my darlings."

"How do you think we're going to get there, Adam?"

"A bus."

"A bus, right." Some of the children weren't paying attention at this point. The teacher said: "Tina and Teresa, we have something to talk about that's very important, and you have to come and listen, so put that away.

"Clap, clap, clap your hands;

"Clap your hands together.

"Clap, clap, clap your hands,

"Clap your hands together.

"Roll, roll, roll your hands,

"Roll your hands together...."

As she sang the song, the children acted out the verbs. They tapped their feet and clapped their hands some more. Craig took off in a direction of his own, neither clapping nor tapping. Mrs. Breitbart said: "Look at Craig! Can you do like this?

"Do, do, do like this;

"Do like this together.

"Do, do, do like Craig;

"Do like Craig together."

She went around the circle, asking the other children to imitate Craig, and then Franklin, and then Adam. Earl tapped his chest; the next child tapped his stomach, and Mrs. Breitbart noticed that some of the children did not know where their stomachs were, and, later, where their shoulders were.

The tapping and clapping song had gotten most of the children into the circle and paying attention, and Mrs. Breitbart moved back into the discussion of the trip to the zoo that she had postponed earlier. She produced a picture of a rooster and placed it on a flannel board in front of the children, singing at the same time:

"I had a rooster, and the rooster pleased me.

"I fed my rooster on a greenberry tree.

"My little rooster went—"

She hesitated, and some of the children made roosterlike noises, but not all of them did.

"—cock-a-doodle-do, de doodle-de doodle, de doodle-de-do."

It was the second time the children had played the game.

Mrs. Breitbart produced a sheep, then a goat, and a cow, then a horse. With the introduction of each new animal, all the previous animals were pointed out, their names repeated, and their sounds imitated by the teachers and the children. Some of the children seemed to have little difficulty remembering the cock-a-doodle-do of the rooster, the baa of the sheep, the naa of the goat, the moo of the cow, and the whinny of the horse. Others had great difficulty, and as the game grew more complicated, with more sounds and names and pictures to remember, they dropped out of the chorus.

"Do you know that we're going to see all these animals at the zoo tomorrow?" asked Mrs. Breitbart. "That's right.

"We're going to the zoo-oo, yes indeed; yes indeed, yes indeed.

"We're going to the zoo-oo, yes indeed; yes indeed, my darlings."

A child shouted: "We're going tomorrow!" Mrs. Breitbart replied, "That's right. Let's everybody sing that.

"We're going tomorrow, yes indeed—we're going *when?*"

A child replied, "tomorrow."

"—tomorrow, yes indeed, yes indeed, yes indeed, my darlings."

"How're we going to get there?" A chorus of children answered, "Bus."

"Right. We're going by bus.

"We're going on the bu-us, yes indeed; yes indeed, yes indeed.

"We're going on the bu-us, yes indeed, yes indeed, my darlings.

"How do the wheels on the bus go?...Round, right. The wheels on the bus go round, round, round...all over town..."

A few minutes later, at 9:30 A.M., Mrs. Breitbart and Miss Jacobson ended the session in the circle and steered the children toward the part of the day that is called *play*. On this particular day, the children were eager to play with the new farm that the teachers had constructed. Three people were allowed to play with the farm at one time. The blocks (nice, smooth pieces of lumber) were also available, along with the doll corner, pasting, the firemen's hats, the doctor's stethoscope, Play-Doh, paints, and the toy store.

Mrs. Breitbart drifted over toward the farm to see how it was being accepted. "This is the silo," she said, pointing out the brick cylinder. "That's where they keep the food for the animals. And this is the barn. This is where they keep all the animals, in the barn. There are the animals; there's a cow, and a turkey, and this is the fence where you can put the animals in the fence. See that? Who's going in the barn?" The child mumbled a reply. "The horse is going into the barn," said the teacher.

Gina had decided to run the toy store that morning. Mrs. Breitbart appeared at the store and asked if it were open. She looked at her make-believe shopping list and ordered some items. The subject came around to money. She suggested that the children make some play money to use at the store. Some of them started drawing circles on paper, then cutting them out. Mrs. Breitbart noticed that only Gina made differently-sized circles to represent nickels, dimes, and quarters; the other children made their money all the same size.

Gina asked if the food that was bought in the store was already hot. Mrs. Breitbart replied: "In a restaurant they make the food get hot. Do you know what a restaurant is, Gina? Do you know what a restaurant is? That's where you can go to get food." Gina smiled: "We got a restaurant here." She pointed to the toilet. "Rest*aurant*," corrected Mrs. Breitbart, "not rest room. That's right."

Mrs. Breitbart stood next to a line of chairs. "Is this the bus going to the store? Where's the bus driver? Is this the bus going to the store? Because I want to go to the store. Will you tell me when we get there, so I can get off? I'll sit over here. I'm on the bus going to the store. You want to come to the store? It's right over there in that block over there....Oh, right; I forgot to pay to get on the bus. Twenty cents for the bus. Oh, this is a bumpy bus. Yes, we're going to the store. Are we there yet, bus driver? Okay, stop the bus; open the door, so we can get out. Thank you."

"Did you ever go to a farm? This is where you keep the food for the animals, called the silo. Just look at this turkey." The miniature turkey, and the other animals, were made of soft plastic. Their features and coloring were intricate and accurate. "Do you see the turkey? Who's in the barn? Who's in the barn? Not the dirt. The dirt's in the box. The animals go in the barn, right.

"Who's in the barn? The cows. This is supposed to be grass, Bobby; you can feed some of the animals grass. Cows eat grass, horses eat grass. This is a pig. Sheep—you can feed them grass, too.

"That's the magnifying glass. That makes things look larger. Look at your name; right. Here, Adam, look at that. What happens? What happens when you use the magnifying glass?" They looked through the magnifying glass at the snapshots of the children that were taped to the front of the lockers. Adam looked at one face and asked, "Who is this?" Mrs. Breitbart replied, "That's Craig." Adam said, "That's not Craig," and Mrs. Breitbart said, "No? Who do you think it is?" Adam looked closer and said "Craig." The teacher said, "Yes, it's Craig."

Back at the make-believe store, Gina was giving Adam a hard time over the make-believe purchase of a bottle of soda. Mrs. Breitbart mediated the dispute. She attempted to interest William in painting. Another child, who had been studying the poster that showed which children would go to the lunchroom to get the milk for snack time, called to Mrs. Breitbart.

"Felicia has what?" the teacher asked. "Today is Monday, and we've got two new people to get the milk." The child said something, not very understandable, and Mrs. Breitbart said: "Oh, is that what you're saying? You think this is Felicia's name? Is that what you're telling me? No, the sign says—" She caught herself, then rephrased her reply. "You know what that says? Can you find out whose name that is? Let's go find out whose name that is." They walked to the line of lockers, where the children's names were printed next to their snapshots. Mrs. Breitbart carried along the name from the milk poster. She and the child compared it to the other names on the lockers. "Is this the same as—Kathy's name? What about Franklin? Yes. So what does it say? Yes, Franklin; that's what it says."

Adam walked over, and the teacher got him interested in cutting some pictures out of magazines. (Most of the magazines used for clipping in the classroom were copies of *Ebony*, and consequently most of the faces and bodies that the children clip out are Negroes, although most of the photographs are considerably lighter than the skins of the children.) A child appeared with a piece of fluffy material in his hand, and Mrs. Breitbart asked him how it felt. "Soft," he said. "Right, soft," she repeated.

The teacher looked back at Adam. He *had* become interested in clipping out pictures, but he was having difficulty with the scissors. (In a white, middle-class pre-kindergarten class, a visitor wondered, would a child have had such difficulty, or would the teacher have been prepared for such a difficulty?)

"That's right, Adam," said Mrs. Breitbart. "Open. Open. Open. And shut. Open, shut. Open, shut. That's right. Now cut this way." Adam started to cut, reciting, "Open, shut." The teacher exclaimed: "That's right! Very good! Now, you want to paste that on to something? To a piece of paper?"

Later, Mrs. Breitbart explained that many of the children

had had trouble in learning to use the scissors, and that one of the underlying difficulties seemed to be that they opened and closed the scissors "so randomly." She said her use of the phrase, "Open, shut," was not so much to tell the child how to open and shut the scissors as it was to establish a rhythm for cutting; once the rhythm was set up, she found, the children had practically no trouble at all.

Across the room, Franklin was establishing a rhythm of his own. He was beating his fist on an empty Quaker Oats box. Mrs. Breitbart hurried over. "Listen to that!" she said. "Franklin, that sounds good. Let me hear that." Franklin responded, but he failed to get the rhythm. "He didn't pick it up," said the teacher later. "I'll have to work more on that."

To a child who was playing with the blocks, Mrs. Breitbart tried to interject the concept of size. Was the block long enough to qualify as a fire truck? To a child who was standing in front of Gina's make-believe store, she tried to stimulate other concepts. "What are you buying in the store?" And to children who were playing with the farm, there was an opportunity to try again to familiarize them with the animals they would be seeing tomorrow at the Central Park Children's Zoo.

"Who's in the barn now? Is the horse going in the barn?" Mrs. Breitbart made a horse sound. A child replied, "It's the cow."

"Is that the cow? That's the bull. Where's the cow? There's the cow. See, you can get milk from the cow."

"Where's the milk?" asked a child.

"These are the udders, see; you can get milk from the cow. And this is the silo, and you can keep food in here for the animals."

"Where's the milk?"

"The milk comes from in here, inside the cow. They pull on

the udders and down comes the milk, from the cow."

"Where's the bowl?"

"The bowl? Okay, we'll get you a bowl. How about using this cup? Is this cup all right? See, the farmer—" the child was pulling at the udders over the cup. "That's good," said Mrs. Breitbart.

It was seven minutes past 10 A.M., and snack time was approaching. Mrs. Breitbart suggested that a child who had been playing with the magnet use the magnet to pick up all the nails and put them away. She talked with the children who were riding the bus to Gina's store; she explained to them about one-way streets, and how the bus would maneuver them, and she was pleased to hear the bus driver ask another child for some gasoline. Bobby, who had been playing with the doctor's tools, approached her with his stethoscope.

"Is this the hospital?" asked the teacher. "I'm feeling very sick today. Can I sit right here? Oh, I'm feeling very weak." The child applied the stethoscope to her.

"How's it sound?' she asked. "Do I sound sick, or—"

"You have to stay in bed," said Bobby.

"I have to stay in bed?"

"Drink coffee and no cake," said Bobby.

"Coffee but no cake? Do you have food in the hospital?... Did you say I need some medicine?"

"Yeah. Medicine every day."

"What kind of medicine?...Do I have any temperature?"

"Yes."

"I do? How do you know?" The child aimed a toy thermometer at her mouth. "Put the thermometer in my mouth? What's the number?"

"One-oh-one."

"Does that mean I have some temperature?"

65

"Yes."

"Can I get up now? I'm feeling much better."

"No, sit down."

The medicine proved to be wooden blocks that the children had borrowed from the block shelf. Mrs. Breitbart suggested that they put the medicine "in the right place so you'll know where it is." She further suggested that they put all medicine of the same size in the same place. ("Putting it back in the right place," she said later, "means putting the blocks into the right place.")

"That's a different kind of medicine; that's a bigger medicine. Find where that goes. Ruth, you can help put some of the medicine back into the drugstore, too. Get all the same size, so you can put it away. That's right...Teresa, come on; we have to put it back before it spoils." (Later, Mrs. Breitbart said she had instantly regretted using the word "spoils." It was obvious, she said, that the children did not know what the word meant.)

Ronald had been playing with the Lego System. The teacher suggested that he put all the red parts in one side of the box and all the white parts in another. "Ronald is a quiet child who stays still," she said later; he required some help at first in sorting out the blocks of plastic.

"Clean-up time, everybody listen," she sang.

"Clean-up time, put the toys away. Thank you, Donald.

"Clean-up time, everybody listen;

"Franklin, too, put the blocks away..."

Is it Sweet?

When it appeared that the children had almost finished cleaning up their toys, Mrs. Breitbart shifted into another song:

"We're going to have snack now, kumbaya.

"We're going to have snack now, kumbaya.

"Earl? We're going to have snack now, kumbaya.

"Adam, put your head down;

"Ruth? Ruth, we're going to have snack now, kumbaya.

"Donald? We're going to have snack now, Donald, kumbaya.

"Deborah? Deborah, we're going to have snack now, kumbaya.

"Oh, Lord, kumbaya...

"We're resting now, kumbaya.

"We are resting now, kumbaya...

"All right, we have something very, very special today," she said, when the children were all sitting at the tables.

"I know what it is," said one child.

"What? What do you think?"

"Applejacks."

"What do you think we're having today?" Mrs. Breitbart asked of the entire group.

"Applejacks," they shouted.

"Applejacks! Does anybody eat these at home? One day you ate it, William? Who else? Did you ever have Applejacks? Donald, did you ever have Applejacks?

"Let's see whose job it is to give out the milk....

"Are you using your bowls today? Oh, you're *not* using your bowls today? The people who are supposed to give out the crackers are giving out the bowls; we don't have crackers today...William, you can open your milk; I saw you do it before; show me now. Bobby, how many straws? Bobby? How many? How many?"

"One."

"Right. Did you use all your milk? Do we have to give out sugar with these, or do these have sugar on them?" There was a chorus of mixed replies.

"Where's the sugar on these?"

"You don't have to put sugar on," said a child.

"You don't have to? Right. Where's the sugar? Tell me if there's sugar on it, Adam. Is it sweet? Is it sugar?"

"Yes."

"Right."

"*Mommy* puts sugar on Applejacks."

"They're *very* sweet. Bobby, what other kinds of cereal do we have in school? Do you remember what kind we had?"

"Corn flakes."

"Corn flakes, right."

"Tall up, tall up," said Franklin.

"Tall up, yes. What's the name of that cereal? Corn flakes?"

"Do you have a white spoon? Is that the same color spoon? What's the color of your spoon? It's white, like mine.

"What did we make at snack the other day, on Friday? You remember what we made? We put some cream in the cup, and we shook it, and what did we make?"

"Butter!"

"Do you remember how we made it? How'd we make it?"

"Shake the cream up and make butter."

"Shake what up? We shook the cream up and it made butter. Is this cream or milk in here?"

"Milk."

It was 10:44 A.M. Mrs. Breitbart asked, "What are we supposed to be doing now? You know what to do; you've done this before. You're going to look at your own books for a while."

The children gathered in the library corner of the room, a small, comfortable rectangle of floor space that was almost surrounded by shelves and books. Some of them went directly to their favorite books. Most of them wanted to be with Mrs. Breitbart as she explained a book about a train to Adam. "Here comes the cat across the track; clack, clickety-clack. What's this? Moooo!"

"A cow," shouted most of the children.

"Here comes the bunny across the track...How many feet does he have, Bobby? One, two, three, four. The bunny does have four legs. This is four. Here comes the pig; oink, oink. Blow the whistle." (A child said "Toot, toot.") "Oh, pig, go back, go back, while the little black train goes down the track."

A child asked if the pig were in danger. "Sure, if he's on the track. That's why they blow the whistle, so he can go back ...Oh, the car on the track. How many wheels?" She counted all the wheels, including the spare. "One, two, three, four— this car has five wheels."

"Six," said one of the children, pointing to the car's steering wheel.

"It has a steering wheel," said the teacher. "That's six wheels; that's right..."

After half an hour, it was time for the children to stop their individual reading (or their listening as the teacher read Adam's book to him) and to sit and listen as Mrs. Breitbart explained a book to all of them. Explained is the correct word here, for the teacher rarely *reads* a book, word for word, to the children.[42]

Mrs. Breitbart opened the book. "Let's see what this book's about," she said. The children, who had seen a picture of a dog on the jacket, made barking sounds. "It's all about a dog named Christopher..." As it turned out, the book was about a dog named Christopher who went to the zoo and got lost; Mrs. Breitbart wasted no opportunities to remind the children that they were going to the zoo tomorrow, and that they were going to see some of the animals that were depicted in

42. The Institute feels that the formal reading of a book to a child is not necessary, especially when it is trying to encourage parents to read to their children.

the book, and that they were going to the zoo on a bus like the one in the book—but that the two buses were not exactly alike. The one in the book was a public bus, and "we're going on a school bus. The school bus is yellow."

There was some discussion of how big elephants were. ("We have some play elephants in the room. But do you think the elephants are really this small?" A chorus of noes. "That's right. They're bigger than you and they're bigger than me.") And, at the end of the book, Mrs. Breitbart reminded the children again. "...and they went out of the zoo and they went home. *We're* going to the zoo.

"We're going to the zoo-oo, yes indeed, yes indeed, yes indeed.

"We're going to the zoo-oo, yes indeed, yes indeed my darlings...Not today; we're going tomorrow.

"Adam get your coa-oat, yes indeed, Craig indeed, yes indeed;

"Earl get your coa-oat, yes indeed, yes indeed my darlings.

"Paula and Ruth and Bobby too, and Franklin too,

"And William, too;

"Teresa and Gina and Deborah too,

"And Ronald and Raleigh, too-oo."

The children and the teachers put their coats on and walked outside to the asphalt playground, where they spent the last thirty or forty minutes of their three-hour school day at play. Even on the playground the teachers did not relax their efforts to teach and ask; one brick is bigger than another, and both of them are hard, not soft. What was soft? A coat collar; was that soft? How high are things, and how do you tell which is taller? Do you remember what we did last time we were here? Do you remember where we're going tomorrow? You do? What noise does the rooster make? The cow? The horse?

The day in the pre-kindergarten class in P.S. 175 may not

70

have appeared radically different from a day in any pre-kindergarten classroom. But the emphases of the Institute's program—on teaching subtle discriminations in size, shape, texture, sound, weight, and taste; on sensitively analyzing each child's individual "deficiencies" and tailoring the intervention program to those individual needs—these were all there.

The materials of an intervention program were there, too, in great numbers. They were materials that are available, by and large, to every school system in the country; the difference was in their selection and their use. The Letter Form Board, for instance, was partially covered so that the children who played with it were not overwhelmed by the presence of twenty-six strange shapes, but rather they were comfortably confronted with seven strange shapes. The stacking rings, too, were ordinary materials, but through the sensitivity of the Institute they had been altered—one set had been painted all yellow.

The small storeroom in the pre-kindergarten class at P.S. 175 offered more evidence of the program's careful attention to the details of an intervention environment. Among the toys and materials in the storeroom were these:

A stethoscope, a wooden toy iron, kaleidoscopes, various Lotto games (Farm Lotto, The World About Us Lotto, Object Lotto, Zoo Lotto, Go-Together Lotto), bottles containing bits of sparkling metal, cork balls, wooden laboratory splints, pots, pans, pipe-cleaner material of various bright colors, plastic bags full of wheels, crayons, Indian corn, and autumn leaves, hats, tempera paints, a doll carriage with a brown-skinned doll, collections of plastic boxes filled with screws, buttons, and peppercorns, magnets, a toy mailbox with variously-shaped slots to admit different blocks, reams of construction paper, plastic trays, pegs, styrofoam balls and other shapes, boxes of clay, drums, and brightly-colored paper in various shapes with glue on the back.

The miniature people used in the children's games are made of rubber, with bendable wire armatures. The dolls at P.S. 175, as the children there, are all Negroes. There is a family, and various other people familiar to the children, such as policemen and firemen.

In the Other Classrooms

As the child advances to kindergarten, and then through the Institute's first-, second-, and third-grade enrichment classes, more and more sophisticated techniques are used to develop and use the stimuli that the Institute hopes have been instilled in the first, pre-kindergarten, experience.

There is not much difference in the classroom materials. The difference lies in how they are used. The tape recorder, which is employed occasionally in pre-kindergarten, becomes a stock part of the classroom by kindergarten. While it may have been used largely as a story-telling device in the pre-kindergarten classroom, it becomes by first-, second-, and third-grade a testing device as well. Children receive instructions on the machine so that they might complete visual tasks. Often, they are encouraged to think up stories of their own, then write them down (on a classroom electric typewriter that has primer-sized type), then record them on the tape in their own voices.

The Institute feels that mastery of language is one of the keys to intervention. Not only does the ability to communicate go a long way toward equipping the slum child for dealing with a world run on middle-class standards; it also gives him a feeling of accomplishment, which means that his concept of himself is improved. So it is not surprising that the major work of the Institute's curriculum supervisors at all the grade levels is concerned with promoting reading and language skills.

The alphabet, first exposed to the children in the pre-kindergarten, becomes more important in the kindergarten year. Mrs. Sandra Bangsgaard, the first-grade curriculum supervisor, said in an interview:

"At the kindergarten level they're using the Letter Form Board, too, but the children are carrying out many other kinds of letter experiences at the same time. They work with letters in different forms. They do a lot of sorting and matching of letters. They work with letters made out of cardboard, letters made out of wood, letters marked on little squares of paper—in as many different forms as possible." One object of this is to show the kindergarten children that a letter may be the *same* as another letter—an A is the same as an a—but that it might *look* different.

"With those children who are ready," continued Mrs. Bangsgaard, "they start learning sounds. This becomes one of the beginning aspects of reading. By the first grade, they're learning many more sounds, and they're combining the sounds into words and then the words into sentences."

The child's progress from letters to sounds to words and sentences, by the way, is ungraded. The Institute has children in the second and third grades of its enrichment program who are reading at kindergarten and first-grade levels, and it has children in kindergarten or first grade who are reading at second-grade levels. This does not disturb the Institute; one of the major aims of the program, after all, is to recognize and provide for the individuality of the children.

At the second-grade level, according to Mrs. Joan Ehren, the curriculum supervisor, "the emphasis is on the child's selecting his own books, knowing what he can accomplish with a particular book, writing reports about the book, making up his own stories, and writing these stories on the typewriter."

By the third grade, said supervisor James Reed, "We hope that the children will be more independent in terms of reading and selecting their reading."

The Institute's attempt to build up children's self-concepts —which started in pre-kindergarten with the emphasis on each child's name, the photographs on the lockers, and the full-length mirror—spreads by the later grades into a program designed to offer the children pride in being Negroes. Harlem residents who are professional people, or who have interesting jobs, are invited to the classrooms to talk about their work. And the Institute is about to embark on an experimental social studies program, part of which involves teacher training in Negro history and the problems of modern-day ghetto life. One of the teachers' textbooks, for instance, will be *Manchild in the Promised Land*, by Claude Brown; another will be *Crisis in Black and White*, by Charles Silberman.

Each of the concepts that were so important in Mrs. Breitbart's pre-kindergarten class—the concepts of size, texture, sweetness, and so forth—play a large part in the curricula of the higher grades, but the part they play is that of a foundation.

"These qualities," said Mrs. Bangsgaard, "are considered part of concept formation. They're pre-math skills, they're pre-reading skills; they're language skills. The curriculum in the pre-kindergarten and kindergarten can focus on areas of auditory discrimination, visual discrimination, concept formation. But when the children get into the grades, these things all merge into reading skills, math skills, and into the usual language skills."

Auditory Discriminations

Much of the Institute's intervention work is based on building up auditory discriminations—discriminations that have been found lacking in the lower-class child, when compared with his middle-class contemporary. One method of trying to cultivate these discriminations is in constant references to rhythm. A child is encouraged to beat out the syllables of his name on a drum, or on a table top (or, in Franklin's case, on a Quaker Oats box); the Institute believes that this is valuable training in the concept of numbers, which soon will become a necessary item in the child's intellectual storehouse. Songs and games like "Adam get your coa-oat, yes indeed," and "Tap, tap, tap your feet; tap your feet together" are played frequently through the school day. In addition to teaching the idea of rhythm, they also help to stimulate the child's memory, another function which has been found to be a victim of "stimulus deprivation."

The storeroom of Mrs. Breitbart's pre-kindergarten class at P.S. 175 has a good number of devices that are designed to stimulate auditory discrimination. In addition to the drums and noise-making toys, there are several records, including albums entitled "Rhythms," volumes one and two, by RCA Victor; "Songs to Grow On," "More Songs to Grow On," a collection of Mary Martin tunes called "Hi-Ho," "Walt Disney Presents Burl Ives Folk Lullabies," "Dance-A-Long," and

"Downtown" by Petula Clark. (Miss Clark's popular rendition of that last song is full of rhythms that encourage foot-tapping, as anyone knows who has watched a group of teenagers who were listening to it on their transistor radios.)

There is a great deal of evidence of the Institute's belief in verbal communication as a means of coping with the problems of the slum child. In the pre-kindergarten class at P.S. 175, there was a set of bright yellow play telephones, which the children use to carry on conversations with considerable imaginative content.

In the Institute's demonstration classes at the *kindergarten* level, a pair of working telephones is used. Dr. Deutsch has expressed the wish that all the classes could have working telephones. The telephone also has been used as a research tool. In the Institute's "Telephone Study," representative speech samples are being obtained from young children "for close study of their verbal behavior—behavior that is especially important for children with serious reading and language difficulties." A pair of classroom telephones is used, with the child on one end and the interviewer and a tape recorder on the other. Telephones are employed in the study because the researchers want to maintain the comfortable setting of the classroom and eliminate any departures from the child's normal way of speaking that might arise from a face-to-face interview with an adult.

In one such study, twenty-two children who had been exposed to the enriched pre-kindergarten program and twenty who had been exposed only to one month of kindergarten were asked general questions over the telephone. The questions, said the Institute, were chosen for their tendency to "elicit and monitor the child's orientation to place and time, his recall of immediate and past events, his labeling ability and imagination in descriptive language usage, and his general ability to communicate verbally." The researchers found that "the children who had received the enriched pre-school curriculum performed consistently better than those in the control group."[43]

In the classrooms where working telephones are used, the Institute has found that even more verbalization on the part of the children may be elicited by placing the phones far apart, or by partially enclosing them and their users in cardboard booths. This cuts down on the children's use of gestures as a means of communication; it thus increases their reliance on the spoken word.

The Institute's "Listening Center" represents another attempt to teach to a child who may have developed the tendency to "tune out." Individual booths, set in corners of the kindergarten and higher-grade classrooms where distractions will be minimal, contain seats and headsets. Children may listen to tape-recorded stories or respond to taped instructions and games through the headsets. Again, the Institute is mindful of the need to pay careful attention to sequence, step size and feedback in the use of the tapes. Again, simple ideas come before complex, and every attempt is made to help the child proceed at a rate that is comfortable and reassuring to him.

One of the ways in which the Institute is trying to produce training in auditory discrimination is through the use of special tape recordings in pre-school, kindergarten, and some of the other classes. "The tapes have sounds that are masked," Dr. Deutsch has written, "so that the child has to pay more and more attention in order to hear what is on the tape. In front of him there are ten or twelve different objects. The objects are mentioned on the tape or the sounds which they make are played, and as they're mentioned the child can

---

43. Institute for Developmental Studies, "Progress Report...", *op. cit.*, pp. 8-9.

reach out and find them.

"More and more masking, more and more overlay of sound is put in the way of a clear delineation of the stimulus so that the child has to listen more and more carefully. This is a technique which seems to work remarkably well in helping children to start distinguishing among sounds."[44]

Most of what goes on in an Institute classroom, from the frequent use of children's names to the thumping of cereal boxes, is directly related to the idea of promoting verbal communication (and, later, the promotion of all sorts of communicative skills). The Institute has suggested, in its report to the Office of Economic Opportunity, that perhaps the noisy (yet nonverbal) environment that characterizes some lower-class homes may provide too small a signal-to-noise ratio (too few meaningful phrases in the midst of too many non-meaningful noises) for the development of adequate auditory discrimination skills. However, both animal and human research suggests that a reversal of this deficit is possible if the child is exposed to clear signals, and is rewarded for responding to them. The enrichment program has attempted to weave a pattern of these necessary signals and rewards into its general curriculum. Specific auditory discrimination goals and the techniques with which to accomplish them have been chosen and introduced into the classroom.[45]

Everything that occurs in an intervention classroom, ideally, is intellectual fodder, an ingredient in the antidote for stimulus deprivation. An ordinary trip to the zoo or the firehouse, a standard item in the repertoire of any pre-kindergarden, kindergarten, or first-grade class, is milked for everything it has. In the case of the firehouse, the concept of size

---

44. Martin Deutsch, "Some Elements in Compensatory Education," *op. cit.*, pp. 6-7.
45. Institute for Developmental Studies, "Progress Report...", *op. cit.*, p. 108

is dealt with by comparisons of the enormous fire trucks and the smaller, ordinary automobile. The shiny fire pole, an object of any child's delight, is used by an alert teacher as a device for explaining speed, and height, and slickness.

When the children who visit the firehouse are Negroes, and Negroes who live in a ghetto, it is important to point out that some firemen are Negroes, at least in some parts of the country. The sight of a Negro fireman, and the bendable rubber Negro fireman back in the toy corner of the classroom, are considered valuable tools in bolstering the child's self-esteem.

When the trip to the firehouse is over, the process of learning from it is far from finished. In Mrs. Breitbart's pre-kindergarten class, the children wrote a booklet about their trip. Made of heavy manila paper and illustrated by the young teacher, the booklet said:

We went to the firehouse.

We saw the fireman.

He slid down the pole. (There was a picture of a Negro fireman sliding down the pole.)

This is the pole.

These are the firemen's boots.

We saw the fire ladder.

Gina made a ladder.

We saw the fire truck.

We got on the truck and rang the bell.

We rang the firebell.

This is a fireman's hat.

Craig wore the fire hat.

Gina and Adam touched the fire hydrant.

This is the hose.

It is on the fire hydrant.

Elsewhere in the room there was evidence that the visit to the firehouse was not forgotten. Several of the boys in the class played almost exclusively with the two plastic firemen's hats whenever there was a chance; ladders had been manufactured out of paper and construction toys. A ladder may be a common household object to a middle-class child, but to a child from the slums, it may be something with which he may not have had direct experience by the time he enters the first grade, unless someone is thoughtful enough to intervene in his environment earlier and teach him its uses.

And that last thought—that someone with the proper qualifications has the thoughtfulness to intervene, and to try to intervene with the proper information and at the proper time —is the most salient feature of the Institute's program. More interesting and obvious than the physical layout of the classroom, more exciting than the abundance of toys and materials in the storeroom, are the dedication and *savvy* of the teacher. And, perhaps, more important than dedication is the awareness that the Institute's sort of teacher has of the situation in which she is teaching. It is the teacher's awareness, and not the blocks and drums, that makes a trip to the zoo or the fire station, a folk song, or the mid-morning snack a mind-stretching experience for the children.

Sensitizing the Teachers

If a visitor to the Institute asks, as the visitors there invariably do, how to go about getting up an intervention curriculum, the Institute's invariable reply is that the first thing to do is to sensitize the teachers. Mrs. Caroline Saxe, the Institute training instructor who is concerned with dissemination of the Institute's findings, is adept at answering questions from interested, but somewhat confused, school officials. She was asked, in an interview, to give advice on setting up a hypothetical intervention program. She replied:

"We have a principal, I assume, who is committed to doing something proper. Let's consider his staff. Probably the first thing he's got to do is to decide whether he's going to use existing staff and retrain them, or whether he's going to build a new staff. Let's say that he's going to retrain staff and look for curriculum development within himself—within the people and resources he's already got.

"All right. Probably the first thing he's got to do is sit himself down with his staff and set himself a set of goals; the kinds of things he wants to happen. I would be inclined to think that the kind of thing he would want would be to build in the skills necessary for reading, writing, and arithmetic, and I would hope that among the goals would be to build a positive self-image in the children themselves, and to involve the parents as part of the school program in doing all of this.

"I think it's important to remember that the child's deficits are not separate and distinct categories that can be treated separately and distinctly. I think that what Dr. Deutsch and the others mean when they say that no one deficit can be treated alone is that any one treatment can be expected to help take care of four deficits, or five deficits. In other words, when you're improving the child's language and making it easier for him to communicate, you're also improving his self-image. Things just don't happen in a vacuum.

"Our hypothetical school administrator would, at this point, have to consider teacher training. And perhaps one of the major responsibilities of teacher training is to give the teacher an idea of the background from which the children come, and her ability to accept these situations without a value judgment—but still to pull the child forward.

"Now, this means a lot of training. If you're dealing with an existing staff, as opposed to hiring an all-new staff, I would suggest that we do some exploration into the types of stereotypes and ideas the existing staff has about children from low socioeconomic backgrounds, and from minority groups.

"And this is not easy. It would take a lot of discussion and a lot of talk about open and frank situations. It might involve some parent visits to homes by the teaching staff. I think it would involve some time being spent by the teaching staff in the community itself....

"The teaching staff would have to become familiar with both the deficits and the existing benefits of the community in which they work. No community is so devoid of services and situations—or, I might say, few communities are so devoid—that there is nothing that would be of positive good. This would be a part of the orientation of the teacher.

"So you spend a lot of time with your teachers in orienting them and trying to find out what their prejudices and stereotypes are. And, then, how do you move them from there? It's not an easy question to answer.

"Ideally, we'd keep up this sort of orientation for years. In the demonstration programs in New York, our teachers meet three times a week. It's not something you can just do and then end. This is part of the whole in-service idea.

"Training the teacher formally would be just one part of the orientation. I think another part would be knowing these things about these children and asking yourself—now that you know what your goals are—what are you going to do? That way, you enter the discussion of curriculum and classroom activities and all sorts of other things.

"For instance, if, as a result of an awareness of the language patterns within a community, you realize that no one around the child expresses feelings in language (it's not 'Please be quiet; I have a splitting headache', but 'Shut up') then you begin to realize that the child's language doesn't get developed, even in the area of expressing his own feelings, so you look for situations in the classroom where there is an opportunity to use language for expressions of feelings, as well as for expressions of needs and wants and other kinds of things. Through this understanding of really what your goal is, at the other end, you're trying to build ways to reach the goals.

"Let's say you're using the Letter Form Board that we're developing. But suppose the child isn't succeeding with the alphabet board. First of all, we have to analyze *why* he isn't succeeding. Is it because his visual perception is poor? Perhaps, instead of complicated letters, we have to start with something even more gross, something that he can handle easily, that he can manipulate and handle before he can go on to the finer concepts. You've got to *go back each time* and find out why he isn't succeeding at each particular task.

"Now, this doesn't mean that the teacher has to use a complicated battery of formal tests every time she wants to analyze why the child isn't succeeding. It's the sort of thing a teacher can do easily. I say, 'Joseph, can you bring me the red pen, please?' and I've got two pens there, and one of them's red and the other is green. After a few opportunities to determine what he *does* know about the situation, I may learn that he does not know how to label red things. Now, that doesn't mean that he doesn't know that it's different from a green thing, but it may mean that he doesn't know the label for a red thing. So I have to go further back and start with him on labeling. Maybe he doesn't see the difference between red and green. So I have to go back and give him a hundred opportunities to match red, to get the *concept* of red, before I even label it."

83

The same approach would be applied, said Mrs. Saxe, to check the child's development in the area of auditory discrimination. She continued:

"I said there were a hundred reasons why he might not have gotten the red pen. Not only might he have the ability to tune out, but also he might be unable to tune into my voice, and my phrasing, and my tempo, all of which are quite different from the voices he hears around his house. It's much more difficult for him to tune in to me than it is for me to tune in to him. So I have to overcome that.

"One thing I can do is to talk at his level physically—not mentally, but physically. I've got to look directly at him when I talk to him, and I can't flood him with language. I have to build in a hundred non-verbal cues for him, because I have to save my language for very important things—because I know he tunes me out.

"Let me give some examples of non-verbal cues. In a certain area of the room we'll have various things on the shelves. Let's say a block of wood so long goes on that shelf.

"We'll have in black Con-Tact paper a reproduction of that block, so I don't have to say 'That's where it goes.' We can make a visual map for these things. That's a non-verbal cue.

"Now, how do I get him to tune *in* to language? You can do it in many ways, and one of the simplest is in a song—a song like 'Old MacDonald Had a—' The child anticipates that something's going to happen. It's a structured situation where he will find that it's to his advantage to listen.

"It stimulates the memory function, too. 'Old MacDonald Had a Farm' is an example of that. Beat your name on a drum. Tom-*mee*. Tom-*mee*. All of these things are play, are fun—but, from the teacher's viewpoint, they're structural; they get the child to tune in. There's nothing nicer than beating your name out on a drum. The teacher can then say,

'Listen: whose name is this?' and beat out a name. And if you don't flood him with the kind of thing that they do so frequently in school—like the old arithmetic problems about the two boys who went out for a walk and one boy had two apples and one boy had three, and so on, and so on—you can have some success. There's a whole variety of ways of telling a story that gets the children to tune in.

"Another structured way to get them to tune in is to place two telephones in a classroom. The teacher dials on the telephone and says, 'I want to speak to Tommy,' and when Tommy comes to the phone the teacher says, 'Tommy, are you in school today? Tommy, tell me where you are....'

"I think what I'm talking about is that it's the *use* to which you put the schoolroom equipment that makes the difference. That doesn't mean you can function without equipment; it means you use it differently. You know, we've had telephones in the classroom since time immemorial, and no one's used them in quite this way. There've been drums in the classroom, too, but the use of drum beats as a means of getting children to tune in has not been used before."

Mrs. Saxe's prescription for an intervention curriculum places relatively little emphasis on the materials that are in the classroom, and relatively heavy emphasis on the teacher who determines how the available materials are used. Again, it is not so much the dedication of the teacher as it is her sensitivity to the children she is teaching.

Sometimes, the Institute has found, teachers may demonstrate a great degree of dedication but they may fall awfully short in their ability to comprehend the difficulties that afflict the lower-class child.

Mrs. Saxe, in spending time in the field with would-be intervention teachers, "trying to find out what their prejudices and stereotypes are," has run across some formidable ones. At

85

one training session for enrichment teachers in a Southern state, she recalled, "I was trying to get the point across, and I said, 'We start with what the child has and you kind of build on that.'

"We were talking about the lack of time orientation, and so forth, in the home of the lower-class child, and one teacher said she had a marvelous program all worked up, and she was going to start with where the children *were* and she was going to *build* things by talking about their homes. 'Now, we're going to talk about their living room,' she said, 'and their dining room, and their bedroom....'

"This was after a week of intensive training, and yet this teacher still wasn't aware of what the inside of one of these children's homes looked like. So we never know quite where we are with stereotypes."

Often, the teachers may be quite sensitive toward the children they teach, and they may have well-formed ideas about how to introduce the stimuli that are missing, but they may find that the pressures of just teaching, or of just trying to hold the classroom together, lead them into other directions. Richard Ellis and Martin Deutsch, in an interview, commented on this when they were asked for examples of successful intervention programs: "The majority of the communities that I've seen," said Deutsch, "have had high aspirations and rather low success, with some exceptions. There are some situations where there has been more progress than others. But, generally speaking, where mass marketing techniques have been applied, there's been an oversell.

"You go to Cleveland, they've got a good program. You go to Houston, they've got a good program. The Atlanta program was quite good. Ypsilanti (Michigan) was excellent. A program in one of the communities outside the University of California at Los Angeles was very good. And there's the

Greeley, Colorado, program...

"The Ypsilanti project particularly emphasized parent involvement. The Los Angeles group emphasized language development. A group in Pittsburgh emphasized discrimination processes. The Cleveland group has emphasized all-around good teaching techniques and an active sort of program, and a lot of input attention. They're doing an excellent, excellent job out there.

"From the research point of view, the Greeley, Colorado, group would certainly be one of the best. Another one is Tallahassee. We're always amazed at the way in which these communities are utilizing our materials, some of them very successfully, some of them in a haphazard way. All of them have the same kind of problems that we have in terms of the tendency of teachers to constantly increase free-play time at the expense of learning time.

"There's a natural tendency, I think—without good supervision and good training and the necessary motivation—for the teacher to be willing to allow the classroom situation to deteriorate into free-play. They aren't conscious of it. Many people are just not aware of it. We've done time counts, and many people have been surprised at the outcome."

Said Ellis: "If we ask any of the teachers, 'Do you read to the children?' they will, without exception, all say 'Yes.' But how often? Frequently? Every day? 'Yes.' And yet our observations show that this is just not so."

"Teachers," said Deutsch, "will keep reporting that they regularly read stories to children—a simple technique that we put a lot of emphasis on. But they don't do as much as they should. Sometimes they read, but they don't *discuss* what they're reading.

"What we're doing is asking the teacher to ask questions of the children. We're asking her to ask, 'What did we hear?

What did Johnny do? Where's the seed planted? Do you remember who planted it? What grew?' It takes listening. And it takes responsiveness. And we have individual teachers who do all this quite naturally. The best teachers will say that this is what happens in a normal classroom situation. But then we go around the country and we don't see it happening anywhere, except where it's kind of forcefully injected."

The Zoo Trip

It takes also a teacher who is intimately aware of the deficiencies of the children she's teaching. It takes a teacher who knows when to ask, "Which of these things do you want to do? Do you want to play with the blocks, or cut out pictures, or play with the fire engine?" and who also knows when to ask, simply, "What do you want to do?" It takes a teacher who sees the possibilities for learning that are inherent in any situation.

Deutsch is fond of expressing this last in terms of the class outing. Every school class takes field trips, he points out; the trick is in making such a trip an educational experience.

"This goes for any time there's a trip, whether it will be to the zoo or elsewhere," he said. "Often teachers will say to children, 'We're going to the zoo, and we're going to see a lot of animals,' and the following Monday they ask, 'Do you remember the trip to the zoo?' and about ten minutes may be spent on it, and that's that.

"Actually, this kind of new experience can be turned into a highly articulated learning situation, involving a great deal of memory retraining and recall, inquiry training, and so forth. You have a calendar; you set out the time that they're going; you color-code the calendar. 'Today's Tuesday; when do we go to the zoo? We go on Thursday. How many days away? Two days away.'

"You have a map of the city. You take a bus. 'How many children are going? How many children are in the class?' You turn left; you turn right. 'Where do we go in the street? What directions? What are some of the major buildings we're going past? What are the major avenues? Do we turn right?' You draw lines on the map, saying 'Here's the school, and here's the zoo; how many turns do we have to make to get to the zoo?' You really build up a picture so it's an across-the-board thing for the internalization of the experience.

"You pay careful attention to the sequence of the thing. And step size. You might say, 'We are first going to see four-legged animals. Then we're going to see the two-legged animals. We're going to see furry animals; we're going to see shorthaired animals; we're going to see reptiles; we're going to see birds.'

"You might have plastic models that the children can identify. Here's a chance to organize them by a dozen different concepts. If you're going to talk about furry animals, you must have a furry animal to use as a model. You can't just use a plastic model that's a poor replication, because this becomes very confusing. You reduce the intake of confusion to an absolute minimum so the child can attend to his various problems.

"When you go to the zoo, you articlate and communicate the various concepts that you've seen. You ask the children, 'Do you remember this?' 'Do you remember that?' 'Do you know where that came from?' You might ask how much they know about money. 'How much did the zoo pay for that animal?

89

What's the most expensive animal? What's the least expensive animal?'

"You come back, and you say 'Where did we go first?' 'Where did we go after that?' 'What did we do?' 'You pick out the animals you saw first.' 'Can you pick out the animals we saw last?' 'What animal did you like the best?' 'What *group* of animals did you like best?' 'What colors did you like?' In other words, you get the child to do a tremendous amount of recall."

A logical question at this point is *where may teachers with this sort of awareness be found?* The Institute for Developmental Studies is not sure it knows the answer to that one, but it thinks it knows where a genuine start might be made.

"There has to be some way," said Ellis, "by which you can sensitize teachers to these kinds of things, because just talking in global terms is not it. The education books of the past have been full of these things. At some point the teacher has to become sensitive to what is going on.

"Now, we talk about making the child conscious of what he is learning. We have to make the *teacher* conscious of what she is doing. Somehow we have to give her certain kinds of skills."

Are these skills born with a teacher, or may they be acquired? Answered Deutsch:

"Let's say that some of them get a little bit of it born into them, and some of them can have it produced in them in the process. I think you have to approach this through the idea of the status of teachers—the levels they're paid at, how you're going to both raise teaching standards and raise the product of the teacher; getting more minority group people involved; getting away from the concept that you can have a two-week training session that will have any new information in it at all; giving teachers, and especially supervisory teachers, at least one intensive year in child development and educational processes.

"I think we're going to have to get away from the concept of free choice as far as the teacher's placement is concerned. We've got to place teachers where they're needed. We get this continual problem where the teacher is just out of school, and they get stuck into the ghetto schools, and they move out to the schools where, if they are good, they are least needed. This is a chronic problem, whether it's a small town in Georgia or New York City or Pittsburgh or Chicago—where the children who need it the most get the least-trained teacher, and as the teacher gets more training she tends to move out of where she is most needed.

"I don't know why we can't develop the capability to do a real retreading job and take some of the teachers back to highly-articulated, in-service, graduate programs lasting one and two years, with a tremendous amount of retraining, and as a result they would get fifty per cent increases in salary, and arrangements could be made so they—this is getting a bit away from reality, I'll admit—so that teachers who become pregnant can have their children, and the children will be cared for under excellent conditions and the teachers can continue in the teaching situation.

"I think that the retreading of teachers can be based simply on the requirement that there be a year or two years of additional training, and that with it comes an automatic increase in status. I'm referring to maybe ten per cent of all the teachers in the country who could be handled like this in five years. Call them 'master teachers,' give them a fifty per cent increment in salary *after* the training, so there's a good deal of competition toward this sort of thing. Then one has to ask oneself where are the training institutions, and I think

91

they're going to have to build themselves up with the demand. They're inadequate now...."

Richard Ellis made the case for sensitive teachers in another way, before a meeting of Canadian and U.S. educators, when he said:

...all of the best philosophy, theory and programming in the world (and there is some trial and error) has little value in the classroom without a good teacher.

What is a good teacher? We don't really know, exactly. It is becoming more apparent, though, that for her to work effectively with young disadvantaged children, she must analyze the experiences she provides the children much more carefully than teachers are accustomed. She must learn to set goals for each child and the group. There are several long-range and many short-term goals that she must state in behavioral terms. She needs a means by which to evaluate her work constantly.

The kind of programming we advocate requires thoughtful analysis, preparation, flexibility, evaluation, and professional thoroughness. This kind of programming requires the efforts not only of teachers or programmers, but also of administrators, supervisors, classroom aides, and parents. The proper task of our educational system is to provide the learning experiences all of our children require.[46]

The Parents

The Institute for Developmental Studies recognized quite early that, while sensitized teachers and revised curriculum were of extreme importance, a planned program of intervention might falter if it failed to incorporate the parents. So a parent program was devised, with its aim the development of "strategies that will help ameliorate the discontinuities that exist between the home and the school, and to develop posi-

46. Ellis, *op. cit.*, pp. 12-13.

92

tive parental attitudes that will lessen future discontinuities between the disadvantaged home and society."[47]

Parents, then are included in just about all of the Institute's plans, hypotheses, and evaluations. Teachers in the experimental programs have revived the old custom of paying visits to their children's home (and it is likely that more than one teacher has learned, graphically, that the children do not necessarily have living rooms, dining rooms, and bedrooms, the way middle-class children do). Parents have been invited to sessions at the school at which they become familiar with the toys and manipulative materials that their sons and daughters play with in the classroom. Discussions are held concerning community problems and the questions every parent has about child-rearing practices; field trips are undertaken to places of interest in the community. (These field trips may be as illuminating to the teacher who is not a native or resident of the community as they are to the parents. "You can't just come in and out of Harlem," said Mrs. Saxe, "and tell what's going on. Do you know, for instance, that there's a very excellent library on One Hundred and Thirty-Fifth Street, the Schomburg Collection [of literature by and about Negroes], and that there's a 'Y' on One Hundred and Seventeenth Street that's open every afternoon for the children in your class?")

Once a month the parents hold meetings with Institute personnel. As might be expected, the chief topics of conversation are the personal, social and economic problems of the parents themselves. An Institute report declares that this sort of approach was encouraged because "it was found that most parents are so concerned with their own problems that they are not able to participate in an academically-oriented program. Also, this approach gives the parents the feeling that

47. Institute for Developmental Studies," Progress Report...", *op. cit.*, p. 156.

93

they, too, are important and that the school's concern is as much for them as their children."[48]

When the social problems of a particular parent are particularly pressing, the Institute's staff attempts to cope with it on an individualized basis, just as the emphasis in the classroom is on individualization.

Parents are hired and used as community aides in the intervention program. The Institute's report to the Office of Economic Opportunity has this to say about community aides:

The addition of community aides, and their ability to supplement the work of the social work staff by interpreting to parents the ways in which they can help their children with the home setting, has significantly increased the effectiveness of the parent program. Aides have been of assistance in the following areas: They have visited the homes to reinforce the learning that has taken place in the parent meetings; they have served as baby sitters, allowing the parent the free time to attend meetings; they have escorted children to school when parents were unable to do so. Because of their unique relationship to the parents and the community, these aides are well qualified to handle certain family problems, e.g., home management and suggestions for improvement in dietary and health problems. Aides have also been extremely helpful in their ability to alert our professional staff to home problems that require special attention.[49]

It is not easy to deal with parents of children who have been labeled "disadvantaged," who are the objects of highly-publicized and nationwide "war," and who *themselves* quite likely are suffering from inferior educations, and undeveloped stimuli, the harsher forms of social and economic discrimination, and the accompanying lack of self-esteem and distrust in anyone who comes along, wearing a white, middle-class face and spending white, middle-class money, and who says he is here to help. The parents, by and large, are distrustful

48. *Ibid.*, p. 158.
49. *Ibid.*, pp. 157-158.

of *anything* that goes on in the school setting.

"The problem for many of the parents," writes Deutsch, "is that they themselves were alienated from school at an early age, and as a result have a certain distrust of the formal education apparatus and have not developed understanding of how school operates."[50]

And, in another context, he has passed along this advice to those who want to intervene:

Many parents feel, 'Why us?...Why are we different? What about our good side?...'

This question keeps coming up, and I think it represents a realistic concern. Many parents recognize that the American society has not been a democratic system for all aspects of American life and for all people in America. One can be very frank with parents in handling this question and in handling prejudice and discrimination. Tell the parent that prejudice and discrimination just are not functional for learning. Tell him that a little extra effort is necessary because he hasn't been reading the kinds of things, engaged in the kinds of jobs, involved in the kinds of activities that are basic to the purposes and goals of the training programs in the schools. The point is, any explanation must be very direct and very explicit. The problem must be dealt with frankly. It cannot be dealt with in euphemisms.

Parents who are on welfare, parents in broken homes, parents who have economic uncertainties, too many children, too much rent, too little room—they know that conditions are not what they should be. This question is often one that relates to the embarrassment and guilt of the middle-class person, both Negro and white, in admitting the defects of American society.[51]

---

50. Martin Deutsch, "What We've Learned About Disadvantaged Children," *op. cit.*, p. 51.
51. Martin Deutsch, "Some Elements in Compensatory Education," *op. cit.*, pp. 13-14.

Does It work?

Does intervention work? Does the sort of enrichment that is formulated and practiced by the Institute for Developmental Studies make a difference when it is applied to the disadvantaged child?

The answer, apparently, is "Yes," with several qualifications. The Institute has been operating its experimental programs since the beginning of the school year 1962-63. It has collected mountains of information on each child in the program—information from standard tests, from the Institute's own instruments, and from its intricate feedback apparatus. It has punched information into computer cards and fed them into machines, and it has arranged the results on charts and graphs and in tables. The overall conclusion that one receives from reading these tables and graphs is that the intervention program is making a positive difference in the lives of the experimental students.

But even now the Institute is reluctant to make sweeping, generalized pronouncements on the quality and effectiveness of its programs. Much more remains to be learned before the Institute will be able to state scientifically that there are direct relationships between particular elements of the curriculum and a child's performance. In that sense, it might be said that the Institute's work has barely started. Among the questions that still need answering are these:

1. Will disadvantaged children, exposed to pre-school and early-grade enrichment programs, attain a significantly higher level of achievement on tests of overall intelligence, verbal ability, concept formation, memory, and perceptual ability than a comparable group of children who are not trained with an enrichment curriculum?

2. Is the enrichment curriculum so effective that it raises the performance level of disadvantaged children so that is indistinguishable from that of middle-class children?

3. How will the intra-individual patterns of performance of experimental subjects, as compared with control subjects, be altered as a result of enrichment?

4. Will short-term differences in achievement continue after enrichment training ceases, and still be *maintained* for one, two, or three years after the initial training?

5. Will lengthening the period of enrichment beyond the pre-school years result in significantly greater post-enrichment achievement?

6. What are the major factors within the enrichment program that account for significant changes in cognitive performance?

7. Can we identify those children who will profit the most from enrichment training through analysis of their pre-enrichment test score patterns?

8. How well can we predict the effectiveness of the enrichment curriculum on children from varying home environments; i.e., what factors in the home environment are associated with patterns of learning?[52]

The answers to those questions will come only after years of study—in what the Institute calls its "long-range longitudinal study within which short-term continuous feedback is available through the use of standardized and Institute-devised and -adapted tests." This longitudinal study will run through 1969.

The short-term results that are now in hand suggest, to the satisfaction of the Institute's experts, that they are heading in the right direction. "Early tests," reported the Institute to the Office of Economic Opportunity, "indicated that definite gains can be achieved in vocabulary and perceptual skills after two years of enriched pre-school and kindergarten curriculum. However, these early gains may be lost if special enrichment is not continued through the first three elementary years."[53]

In a less formal situation, Martin Deutsch has described the success of the program more dramatically. Speaking to a group of educators, he said:

Some of the very disadvantaged children that we have in our experi-

52. Institute for Developmental Studies, "Progress Report...", pp. 61-62.
53. *Ibid.*, p. xviii.

mental school program are doing as well at the end of the pre-school year as we had predicted they would at the end of the first grade. They received a lot of individual attention, but the point is that the children are capable of learning; they are motivated.

What has been done was to give them a good many success experiences. And they were given a lot of opportunities for verbalization in all procedures. For example, in a number of games we ask the child to tell a story, and we say, 'When you tell your story, will you mention the ball, the tricycle and the book?' The child will then feel the experience of trying to put these three categories together. Or one might be interested in the problem of transportation. Ask the child to tell a story mentioning an automobile, a bicycle and a boat....

The point is that one gives the child opportunities to manipulate aspects of the environment that he can handle. If he does a poor job, and doesn't include all the objects, then he does it the next day, or the day after. At no time does one insult a child by overpraising another child's capabilities and ignoring the first child's response. As the teacher becomes aware of a child's particular level, she indicates that she appreciates it. The basic measurement should not be a competitive comparison, particularly when dealing with these childen. Do not ask how this child functions in comparison with the middle-class child. Rather ask how this child functioned with this kind of problem four weeks ago and how does he function now....[54]

And Deutsch added more recently in an interview, when asked about the effectiveness of the intervention program:

"There is absolutely no question that it is working. If it's working *sufficiently?* That's something else. There's absolutely no question that the degree of influence is insufficient; that the children have a great deal more capability than we assign them; that the school system continually sabotages their progress; that the total bureaucratic nature of the social organization—the American community and the American schools—acts as another source of sabotage. And yet, at the same time, the children make progress in spite of all this.

"I think a lot will happen if we can maintain, as I keep re-

54. Martin Deutsch, "Some Elements in Compensatory Education," *op. cit.*, pp. 12-13.

peating, *continuity.* Keep the same teachers, the same data, the same files, and keep changing it at the same time—keep changing it in a creative way and keep giving children new chances."

One of the short-range instruments that the Institute has used to evaluate its work has been the Illinois Test of Psycholinguistic Abilities, better known, by those who have to refer to it often, as the ITPA. The test, developed by psychological researchers at the University of Illinois, charts ability in the fields of language, perception, and cognition. It consists of nine subtests, each of them designed to measure one function that relates to the language development in children.

The Institute started using the ITPA test on its children when the first group of experimental students was in the first grade. The test has been repeated, on the experimental group and on control groups, at the beginning of the second grade, and then at the beginning of the third grade.

The Institute has found that on virtually all of the component subtests, the children who received the enriched eduation scored higher than did the control group. Cynthia Deutsch, wife of Martin Deutsch and one of the Institute's senior research scientists, commented in an interview: "On the basis of the ITPA data we can say that the experimental children are consistently above the control group on all subtests. Now, this does not mean that all of those differences are statistically significant. The overall difference is statistically significant in each year. Unfortunately, some of the second- and third-year differences appear to have occurred not because the experimental groups have gained so much but because the control group has lost—which fits in with the idea of the cumulative deficit."

The Institute has noted that, in the data obtained from the

Illinois tests, both the experimental children and the control group children followed the same patterns of performance—but that the enriched children scored consistently higher. Rough graphs of the ITPA results for the years 1964, 1965, and 1966 clearly demonstrate this, as can be seen on the following pages."[55]

ITPA MEAN SCORES, BY SUBTEST[55]

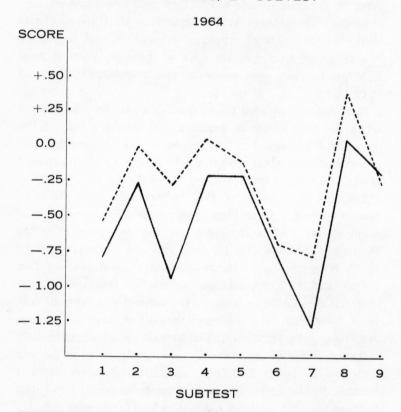

1964

SCORE

SUBTEST

55. Adapted from "Tenth Quarter Progress Report: Patterns of Perceptual, Language, and Intellective Performance in Children with Cognitive Deficits," Institute for Developmental Studies, Cynthia P. Deutsch.

1965

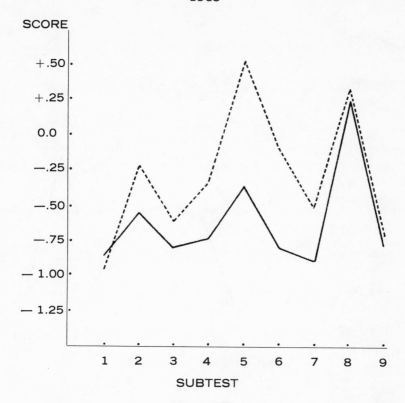

SCORE

+.50
+.25
0.0
—.25
—.50
—.75
— 1.00
— 1.25

1   2   3   4   5   6   7   8   9

SUBTEST

———————— CONTROL GROUP
------------------- EXPERIMENTAL GROUP

SUBTESTS: 1. AUDITORY DECODING
            2. VISUAL DECODING
            3. AUDITORY VOCAL ASSOCIATION
            4. VISUAL MOTOR ASSOCIATION
            5. VOCAL ENCODING
            6. MOTOR ENCODING
            7. AUDITORY VOCAL AUTOMATIC
            8. AUDITORY VOCAL SEQUENCING
            9. VISUAL MOTOR SEQUENCING

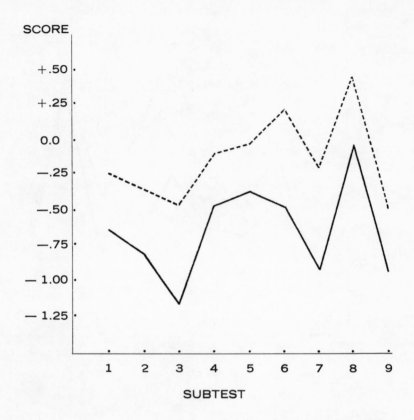

1966

SCORE

SUBTEST

Other testing instruments that are being used by the Institute to measure the effectiveness of its programs include the Stanford-Binet Intelligence Scale, which measures intelligence and is a highly reliable test for pre-kindergarten-age children; the Peabody Picture Vocabulary Test, which measures a child's ability to connect a verbal label to its visual counterpart (the child chooses, from among four pictures, the one that corresponds to the verbal cue); and the Columbia Mental Maturity Scale, which checks on the child's conceptual abilities and his "ability to organize visually perceived stimuli."

The children who have been taking these tests have been classified into four categories:

The *experimental* children [E in the Institute's records and tables], whose parents sought admission to the Institute program, and who have been attending the Institute's enriched classes at pre-kindergarten, kindergarten, first-, second-, or third-grade level.

The *self-selected control group* [C_{ss}], children who meet the criteria of the experimental group, and whose parents applied for admission to the program, but who were selected at random to serve as controls. They do not receive enriched education.

The *kindergarten controls* [C_k], who are children from the same backgrounds as the experimental and self-selected controls, and who have no previous nursery or kindergarten experience, and who start their education with kindergarten, in regular schools.

The *first-grade controls* [C_1], who are children from the same backgrounds, who have had no school experience, and who start their education in regular, non-enriched first grade classes.

Tests have shown that, for the children who entered the

intervention program in the academic year 1962-63, pretests given all students revealed little or no significant difference in scores among the four categories. After one year of en- richment for the E child, a test was given. The scores of the E children were higher. After the second year, the difference, as measured by the Columbia Mental Maturity Scale, seemed to diminish. On the Peabody Picture Vocabulary Test, *only* a "weak treatment effect" was observed at the end of the second year. It was noted by the Institute that at the beginning of the testing of the 1962-63 group, the children were of different ages. By the time of the second post test, all the children who were tested were of approximately the same age.[56]

Other tests, on children who entered the program in the academic years 1963-64, 1964-65, and 1965-66, tend to give similar results. There is a significant improvement in the E children after their first year of exposure to the program. Improvement frequently is noted, too, in the C_{ss} children by the time of their second pretest. There is considerable evidence, though, that the child who begins school last (the C_1 child on the Institute's charts and tables) is at a real disadvantage. This would tend to reinforce the Institute's cumulative deficit hypothesis.

Dr. Leo Goldstein, who is one of the senior research scientists at the Institute for Developmental Studies, commented in an interview on the results that presently are in hand:

"We're now in the fifth year of the program," he said. "I always say, when I'm talking about this, that these are early findings. And I want to stress this, because this is a longitudinal study. These are findings relating to the first two years' evaluations of each of these groups. We consider the first two

---

56. In addition to the test data, there are many less formal evaluation data being collected. These include teacher observations and reactions, application of observation scales to teachers' and children's behavior, parental reports and reactions, and the like.

years as pilot groups, so to speak. We consider them pilot groups, really, because all the time they were in the program we were exploring the kind of curriculum to use with these children.

"The third-year group—that is, the children who are now in the first grade—I would consider as really the first non-pilot group. But this is not to say that we have now reached the point where we have a fixed curriculum. This is not true. The curriculum is in a constant state of evolution. Perhaps the change isn't as rapid as in the first two years, but we are still looking for those elements which will improve the curriculum, whether they be at the pre-kindergarten level, the kindergarten level, or all the way through. And therefore this whole study is different from a finely-controlled laboratory study.

"We have here a study that's in the field, in which there are elements which we cannot control, like a changing experimental treatment. It becomes difficult to say what part of the curriculum is causing what changes that we have been able to measure as a result of the evaluation. That's one reason why we're loath to do too much generalizing from these early findings."

Dr. Goldstein spread out before him three tables of numbers. The tables reflected the Stanford-Binet IQ scores of children who entered the program in 1963-64. They included these statistics:

GROUP	Pretest scores for all groups	First Post-test for E and C_{ss} children; same pretest for C_k, C_1	Second Post-test for E and C_{ss} First post-test for C_k; same pretest for C_1
E	93.32	99.02	95.53
C_{ss}	94.69	92.48	96.52
C_k	88.21	88.21	90.33
C_1	80.86	80.86	80.86

105

Dr. Goldstein looked at the left-hand column of figures, the children's scores on their pretests, and compared them with the scores in the center column, which were obtained one year later, after the E children had finished one year of pre-kindergarten classes. "The experimentals," he said, "have gained. The self-selected controls have dropped about two points—statistically significant; nothing to shout about, but still it's statisticaly significant. The E children have had schooling, but none of the others have. The differences between the groups are statistically significant."

He pointed at the right-hand column. "The difference here is that the C_1 children, those who enter school at the first grade, have an average performance which is significantly poorer than that of the other three groups. There is no significant difference among the three other groups—among the self-selected controls, the kindergarten controls, and the experimental group. Their means are not significantly different. But all their means are significantly higher than those of the C_1s—the children who 'start school later,' so to speak. This is an indication of what we call the cumulative deficit.

"Now, why is it that we do not get a difference for this group in favor of the E children as we did for the first year's group? I cannot explain it. I don't know. I know that they're not doing significantly *poorer* than the control groups, which is fine, but they're not doing significantly better, either. That's all I can say. It's difficult to make an interpretation. Because I don't know what happened to the curriculum then."

Dr. Goldstein said he did not want to venture any guesses as to what element of the curriculum might have caused the experimental group's advantage to disappear. "We do know," he said, "that these three groups—the E, C_{ss} and C_k groups— have had some schooling, and apparently schooling makes a difference, because those kids who begin schooling at first grade have not had any school experience at the time of this testing, and you see that that they are performing significantly poorer. So, apparently, any kind of school experience is good for the child."

Dr. Goldstein's visitor asked if a skeptic might not interpret the tables as showing that the Institute's intervention program didn't work.

"No," he replied, quickly and loudly. "What do you mean when you say 'work'? When I say 'work' I'm talking about long-term programs—five years of programs. These are short-term results.

"It's a good question, but my hackles go up when I hear it because it would be funny if it worked for the first year and not for the second. And that's what those tables show. I don't know what happened in that second year that made the difference."

As for skeptics, he said, "if they have expectations that giving children nine months of enrichment at the prekindergarten level is going to have a profound and lasting effect, they're kidding themselves. It *will* have an effect. It will have an immediate effect that will last for a couple of weeks. You pay your money and you get what you pay for.

"We know, with kids who attend 'regular' classes, that at the end of the third grade a goodly proportion of them are a year retarded in reading ability. At the end of fifth grade, a goodly proportion are two years retarded. At the end of sixth grade, three years retarded. Now we want to see what happens with our experimental kids. I want to see these kids at the end of third grade, and I want to look at them again at the end of fourth grade, and fifth. I want to see if there's an immediate positive effect at the end of third grade, and I want to see if they're different—significantly better—than their age peers who have not had any enrichment.

"Does being in regular classes goof up everything that's happened to them in the five years of enrichment, or are they able to maintain their performance with this five years of experience bolstering them? I think they will.

"I anticipate that they will maintain their lead. I will make a direct hypothesis that the children who experience five years of Institute-enriched classes will maintain their 'superiority' on various measures of achievement over those children who have not had enriched classes, who have been in regular public school classes."

Relevant to this, the Deutschs maintain:

Another element to be considered in evaluating the effects of special programs is time. There is no reason to suppose, *ipso facto*, that all effects will be immediately visible, nor that immediate gains will be maintained. It is possible that continuing enrichment programs in the elementary years will be necessary if these gains are not to be lost. It is highly likely that certain functions need a long time to mature once they are stimulated, while others develop at a fairly rapid rate. It is also likely that some curricula will stimulate development in areas which seem far removed from the content. Further, it is eminently plausible to assume that stimulation of a basic function at a time later than that at which it would ordinarily develop might not automatically yield the consequent development of the more specific skills which it underlies. Many similar questions can be formulated, all pointing to the necessity of an evaluation over time in order to ascertain the effects of an intervention program: to yield the information of which it is capable, evaluation must go on over a period of years.[57]

Later information on the performance of the third-year group became available as this report was being completed. At the end of the school year, these first graders and their controls were given the Gates MacGinitie Vocabulary test, a standardized reading test. The Institute children, who had received three years of enrichment program, averaged eight

57. Cynthia P. Deutsch and Martin Deutsch, "Brief Reflections on the Theory of Early Childhood Enrichment Programs," prepared for the Social Science Research Council Conference on Early Childhood Education, Chicago, Ill., p. 10.

months higher score than their controls. This represents a statistically significant difference in reading achievement between the experimentals and the C_{ss} group at the end of first grade. The average score achieved by Institute first grade children was above national norms.

Dr. Deutsch reported: "Described by Dr. Goldstein as the first 'non-pilot' group, these are the children whose performance is beginning to reflect the changes in curriculum and teacher training which were developed during previous 'pilot' years. A very encouraging trend seems to be emerging. Children coming from pre-kindergarten classes where innovation in curriculum has been established are making significant progress during their first year in the grades, when continued curriculum, ongoing supervision, and in-service teacher training is provided."

There is every reason, then, to believe that the Institute for Developmental Studies is heading in the proper direction with its plans for intervening massively in the lives of disadvantaged children—armed with its tests, hypotheses, feedback mechanisms, detailed research and followup, its cans of yellow paint that are used to make stacking-rings uniform, its attention to the shape and sweetness of breakfast cereal, its search for teachers who are sensitive and its parallel search for ways to make other teachers more sensitive.

In its nine years of existence, the Institute has not run across any magical solutions to the problems of the disadvantaged child. But it is starting to build some practical approaches, and a growing body of educators and scientists is paying attention to what the Institute is building. The progress of the children who are enrolled in the Institute's experimental programs is being charted with minute precision by Dr. Goldstein and the rest of the staff, but it also may be reflected in other ways. There was Mrs. Breitbart's excitement over "My Mommy and my Daddy took me," the longest sentence one of her children had ever spoken in her presence. And there is the comment from Sandra Bangsgaard, the Institute's first-grade curriculum supervisor, to a group of visiting (and probably somewhat skeptical) school administrators:

"After two years," she said, "the children have some of the same problems they had before. But the children also have learned to use the adults as resource people. They have become a group that's verbal, that communicates their desires. They still have difficulty getting out exactly what they want, but there's no hesitation in trying. They respond more to questions. The children *have* ideas. They're relatively confident in the school setting. They're accustomed to freedom of movement in the school classroom.

"It's a demanding group—as demanding as a teacher might find in a private school. This, of course, presents problems. But it's what we want."

About the author

Fred Powledge, most recently a race relations reporter for *The New York Times* in the South and North, has also worked for the Associated Press, *The Atlanta·Journal*, and various southern newspapers. He has written articles for *The New Republic, The New Yorker, Life,* and *Esquire,* among other leading magazines. His book, *Black Power—White Resistance: Notes on the New Civil War,* was released in 1967 by the World Publishing Company.

Mr. Powledge was a Russell Sage Fellow at Columbia University, where he studied the behavioral sciences. He is now a free-lance writer, specializing in race relations, civil rights, civil liberties and the social revolution.